biobest®

SUSTAINABLE CROP MANAGEMENT

Biobest Nort

@1BIOBEST

Biobest North America • Tel: (519) 322-2178 • Toll free: 1-855-224-6237 • Fax: (519) 322-1271 • customerservice@biobest.ca • www.biobestgroup.com

Enhancing Profitability in Greenhouse Firms

Edited by:
Charles Hall — University of Tennessee

Contributing Authors:
Susan Barton — University of Delaware
Bridget Behe — Michigan State University
Robin Brumfield — Rutgers University
Charles Hall — University of Tennessee
Richard Harkess — Mississippi State University
Charles Safley — North Carolina State University
P.J. van Blokland — University of Florida

Natural Resource, Agriculture, and Engineering Service (NRAES)
Cooperative Extension
PO Box 4557
Ithaca, New York 14852-4557

NRAES–164
June 2005

ISBN 0-935817-95-6

Library of Congress Cataloging-in-Publication Data

Enhancing profitability in greenhouse firms / edited by Charles Hall ; contributing authors, Susan Barton…[et al.].
p. cm. — (NRAES ; 164)
Includes bibliographical references.
ISBN 0-935817-95-6 (pbk.)
1. Greenhouse management—Economic aspects—United States. I. Hall, Charles. II. Barton, Susan S. (Susan Schumacher). III. Natural Resource, Agriculture, and Engineering Service. IV. NRAES (Series) ; 164.

SB415.5.E54 2005
635.9'823—dc22

2005041669

Natural Resource, Agriculture, and Engineering Service (NRAES)
Cooperative Extension
PO Box 4557
Ithaca, New York 14852-4557
Phone: (607) 255-7654
Fax: (607) 254-8770
E-mail: NRAES@CORNELL.EDU
Web site: WWW.NRAES.ORG

Contents

Acknowledgments

This book was peer reviewed for technical accuracy. The authors would like to thank the following for offering comments to improve the quality and accuracy of this book.

Robert G. Anderson
Professor
Department of Horticulture
University of Kentucky

John W. Bartok, Jr.
Consulting Agricultural Engineer
Ashford, Connecticut

John R. Brooker
Professor
Department of Agricultural Economics
University of Tennessee

Warren Goll
Multi-County Horticulture Agent
Penn State Cooperative Extension

Robert E. Graves
Professor
Department of Agricultural and Biological Engineering
The Pennsylvania State University

Alan W. Hodges
Assistant-In
Department of Food and Resource Economics
University of Florida

Joyce G. Latimer
Professor
Department of Horticulture
Virginia Polytechnic Institute and State University

David S. Ross
Professor and Extension Agricultural Engineer
Department of Biological Resources Engineering
University of Maryland

Michael R. Sciabarrasi
Extension Professor/Business Management Specialist
Department of Resource Economics and Development
University of New Hampshire

Forrest Stegelin
Associate Professor
Department of Agricultural and Applied Economics
University of Georgia

Wen-fei L. Uva
Senior Extension Associate
Department of Applied Economics and Management
Cornell University

Daniel Warnock
Associate Professor
Department of Natural Resources and Environmental Sciences
University of Illinois

Jay Windsor
Extension Educator Emeritus/Horticulture
Research and Education Center
University of Delaware Cooperative Extension

Dennis J. Wolnick
Associate Professor Emeritus of Floriculture
Department of Horticulture
The Pennsylvania State University

This book was copyedited by Cathleen Walker, NRAES production editor. Holly Hyde, NRAES editorial assistant, managed the peer-review process. Many thanks to Andrea Gray of Burlington, Vermont, for creating an attractive, thoughtful design.

About the Authors

Susan Barton
Extension Specialist/Ornamental Horticulture
Department of Plant and Soil Sciences
University of Delaware

Bridget Behe
Professor
Department of Horticulture
Michigan State University

Robin Brumfield
Extension Specialist/Farm Management
Department of Extension Specialists
Rutgers University

Charles Hall
Professor
Department of Agricultural Economics
University of Tennessee

Richard Harkess
Associate Professor
Department of Plant and Soil Sciences
Mississippi State University

Charles Safley
Professor
Department of Agricultural and Resource Economics
North Carolina State University

P.J. van Blokland
Professor
Center for Entrepreneurship and Innovation
University of Florida

S-290 Multistate Regional Project—Cooperating Agencies and Principal Leaders

Cooperating Agency	Principal Leaders
Auburn University	Deacue Fields, Joe Eakes,* Ken Tilt
Cornell University	Wen-fei Uva
University of Delaware	Susan Barton*
University of Florida	John Haydu,* Alan Hodges, P.J. van Blokland
University of Georgia	Forrest Stegelin, Steven Turner*
University of Illinois	David Williams,* Daniel Warnock
University of Kentucky	Robert McNiel*
Louisiana State University	Jeff Kuehny, Roger Hinson*
Michigan State University	Bridget Behe,* Tom Fernandez
Mississippi State University	Patricia Knight, Richard Harkess,* Ben Posadas
North Carolina State University	Charles Safley*
Rutgers University	Robin Brumfield*
The Ohio State University	Hannah Mathers*
Oregon State University	Larry Burt*
The Pennsylvania State University	Dave Beattie *
Purdue University	Bruno Moser*
University of Rhode Island	Brian Maynard*
University of Tennessee	John Brooker,* Charles Hall
USDA/CSREES	David Holder
Administrative Advisor	D.C. Coston

*Official Voting Member

1 Issues Affecting Profitability of the Greenhouse Industry

Charles Hall—University of Tennessee

One of the key premises in strategic management is the identification of principal driving forces (or trends) that affect the industry in which you are competing. "Driving forces" move to create incentives or pressures for change. The most dominant driving forces will have an impact on the kinds of changes that will take place in the industry's structure and competitive environment. Managers will not really understand industry and competitive conditions until they understand the fundamental drivers of change.

For the past few years, data have been collected and analyzed regarding the most dominant driving forces that will affect the greenhouse industry at all levels of competition. In fact, several workshops were focused on identifying such driving forces. At these sessions, various growers, landscapers, and retailers worked hard in brainstorming and summarizing what they felt were the key driving forces that the greenhouse industry will have to face in upcoming years.

As a preface to the findings, an interesting point was noted regarding driving forces of change: No one knows exactly what's going to happen in the future. Forecasts and predictions, even those made by "experts," are oftentimes unreliable, as they tend to be based on extrapolation and projection. This exposes them to two killer caveats—"if present trends continue" (they never do) and "all other things being equal" (they never are).

It sounds daunting, but one can begin to identify and categorize the driving forces or trends that are relevant to one's own business. For a greenhouse professional in today's competitive environment, these trends include:

- **Social/lifestyle/consumer trends.** Are middle-aged consumers trading down and buying less as they reevaluate their priorities? If so, is this temporary or permanent? If not, is there a switch to shopping for and purchasing goods in a more price-conscious manner?
- **Business/management trends.** Will slow, uneven growth continue through the rest of the decade? Who will be the winners and losers, and what will determine success or failure in an uncertain era? What technologies will be most important for growers to adopt in the future?
- **Political/legislative/regulatory trends.** What laws will be passed on the federal, state, or local level that will affect my business, customers, employees, suppliers?
- **Workforce/workplace trends.** Can I find and retain employees with the skills and motivation needed at salaries I can afford? How do I supervise them while giving the right level of autonomy and responsibility?
- **Marketing/advertising/media trends.** How do I reach today's more segmented, fragmented marketplace? What message do I want to convey?

Should I compete on price, service, selection of merchandise, quality, convenience, or a combination thereof?

Can these questions really be answered in a definitive and absolute way? Not really. But definitive answers are not the point. More important is the process of considering the future and the acknowledgment that it will be different from the past and present. Conducted thoughtfully and imaginatively, this process can become a strategic tool that enables its practitioners to be prepared for whatever the future may bring. And that is indeed the point.

When brainstorming regarding these driving forces in focus-group settings, participants came up with several dozen possible ideas. After combining related ideas to reduce duplication, five major categories of driving forces emerged:

- Environmental concerns are increasing
- Regulatory concerns are increasing
- Communications technology is improving
- Customers are consolidating and becoming more sophisticated
- Partnership marketing is increasingly emphasized

However, identifying the driving forces is only the first step. Assessing their potential impact on the greenhouse industry and proposing possible solutions or actions that deal with these driving-force impacts is the next step. These impacts and proposed solutions are summarized in the sections that follow.

Driving Force #1

Environmental Concerns Are Increasing

Impact on Industry

- Demand for environmentally "friendly" plants will increase.
- Use of native plants and organic gardening will increase.
- Availability of chemicals and chemical use will change.
- Suppliers and manufacturers will either adapt or "fall off" approved-vendor lists of retailers.
- More research will be conducted on chemical use, plant varieties, genetically modified plant materials, etc. (i.e., aesthetic versus economic thresholds).
- Efforts to recycle plastic films, trays, and containers will increase. (Composting will increase as well.)
- Water conservation efforts will affect plant selection, greenhouse size, etc.
- Pressure will mount on municipal landfills due to increasing volume of yard-waste deposits.
- The industry will have to stay on top of key legislative issues as they arise.
- Water quality concerns will change how water is used and how runoff is managed.
- Chemical manufacturers (and growers) will be encouraged to take more responsibility in the disposal of "toxic" materials.

Proposed Responses

- Set up environmental "hotline" at the retail level.
- Use public relations to help educate the public on environmental stewardship.
- Ensure that merchandising at the retail level has an environmental "flavor."
- Offer "unbiased" recommendations at the retail level.
- Train or even certify staff at all levels (may need an expert on staff).
- Increase product mix to include native, xeriscaping products and environmentally friendly products.
- Recycle water at all levels (grower and retail).
- Set an example in display landscapes.
- Offer seminars in environmental stewardship.
- Encourage promotional programs such as "Don't-Bag-It" to reduce yard waste in landfills.
- Promote composting by providing information at the retail level.
- Emphasize recycling of used containers.

Driving Force #2

Regulatory Concerns Are Increasing

Impact on Industry

- Irrigation legislation will increase at city, county, and state levels.
- Increased pressures on minor-use chemicals will

increase costs of registration.

- Worker-protection legislation will increase labor costs in the short run.
- Research regarding pest control will increase (e.g., alternatives to chemicals).
- Chemical disposal methods at the grower, retail, and consumer levels will be reviewed and monitored.
- International competitiveness will be affected.
- More paperwork will be required.
- Plant-production processes may change as well as the composition of the workforce.
- Insurance rates will increase as the extent of liability increases.

Proposed Responses

- Stay positive and active at the association level.
- Acquire information faster.
- Training, training, and more training!
- Be proactive, not reactive.
- Write letters to government officials.
- Hire outside companies for spraying (outsourcing).
- Support research projects at land-grant universities.
- Develop educational programs on health and safety regulations.
- Develop educational programs on environmental regulations.

Driving Force #3
Communications Technology Is Improving

Impact on Industry

- The Internet will increase availability of production and marketing information (at home, in the store, for the grower, etc.).
- Scanner data will be used to measure customer buying preferences (efficient consumer response—ECR), especially with supermarket loyalty programs. Such data will also generate more precise and faster summary/analysis of promotional efforts.
- Partnerships will be encouraged between suppliers and vendors using electronic data interchange (EDI).
- Plant labeling will be easier (providing information regarding culture, price, etc.).
- Speed of communications will increase.

Proposed Responses

- Develop a long-range plan on how to manage communications.
- Provide computer literacy training (in-home and outside) to stay up-to-date on the latest technology.
- Update existing computer systems.
- Learn how to use the Internet for conducting business-to-business (B2B) commerce.
- Implement point-of-sale (POS) systems to track customer sales.
- Utilize CD-ROM information systems to provide advice regarding insect control, plant selection, etc. Use digital cameras to quickly "image" a pest or problem to send via Internet or fax to problem solvers.

Driving Force #4
Customers Are Becoming More Sophisticated

Impact on Industry

- Customers are demanding service at all levels of the value chain.
- Customers are demanding knowledge and information.
- Demographic shifts may dictate alternate marketing strategies (regarding retirees, elderly).
- Apartment dwellers will need more shade-loving and blooming annuals/perennials.
- Opportunities exist to expand the customer base.
- Customers are becoming more aware of their "choices" (of stores, plant material, information sources, etc.).
- Customers want to spend less time shopping (in general).
- Advertising will need to be more creative and stimulating.
- Self-service shopping will influence purchasing methods.
- There will be continued emphasis on "microwave" gardening—instant landscapes that have reduced maintenance.
- Customers will be interested in alternative landscapes (water gardening, xeriscape, organic, etc.).

- There will be more of a need for niche marketing.
- There will be a need to discern taste and preference trends affecting local trade areas.

Proposed Responses

- Offer concessions and "related" services at the garden center.
- Ensure that employees are well trained and knowledgeable.
- Implement stronger customer-service programs to build long-term customer support.
- Pay attention to image and reputation.
- Growers and seed dealers need to constantly update/improve plant varieties, packaging, and shipping systems.
- Offer value-added products.
- Ensure a pleasant shopping experience (atmosphere, layout, etc.).
- Offer seminars on pertinent topics.
- Implement mail order (home shopping) and home delivery services (be convenient).
- Use cooperative advertising between growers and retailers.
- Offer computerized in-store information systems (insect/disease identification, pictures of plants in bloom, etc.).
- Hire knowledgeable employees (i.e., master gardeners, certified greenhouse professionals).
- Set up a toll-free phone information line.
- Sponsor a "Future Gardeners of America" program for local schools.
- Work collectively as an industry to compete for leisure-time dollars of customers.

Driving Force #5
Partnership Marketing Is Increasingly Emphasized

Impact on Industry

- Fewer vendors (suppliers) will appear on approved-vendor lists of retailers.
- Paperless ordering systems (EDI) and ECR tied to scanner data at the retail level will generate more "in-advance" contract orders.
- Vendors will become stratified between mass merchandisers and independents.
- Better inventory-control management will be possible at all levels in the industry (will be able to service customers better).

Proposed Responses

- Use night docks in shipping.
- Improve in-transit communications (cell phones).
- "Lease out" departments in the garden center—i.e., growers become "jobbers."
- Implement more sophisticated plant labeling and bar coding systems.

Concluding Thoughts

After considering this evaluation of the driving forces affecting the industry's operating environment and where it could be heading, it is time to determine a future strategy. Leaders within the business must look deeply into the core of the business and themselves and decide what role they want to play. What is the purpose of the business? The goal? What is its claim to the marketplace? Who is to be served? What is the strategic intent of its stewards? How do they envision its future in the possible environments described by the scenarios?

Many growers (large and small) have gone through the process of attempting to understand the future and developing new strategies to fit it. The task is not a simple one, and those who have undertaken it have experienced varying degrees of success. During the last two decades, several leading firms saw their traditional markets moving away from them. They took a hard look at their futures, redefined their missions, and implemented vast changes. Some firms rode a tremendous wave of initial popularity but failed to anticipate changes in consumer desires and buying habits and are still playing catch-up. Others saw an opportunity in going national and are now exploiting that opportunity. Still others saw an opportunity in going international and will be moving into developing markets over the coming years.

The goal of these efforts should be to develop a proactive business—one that anticipates, even foresees, challenges and opportunities; one that is responsive, not reactive, in dealing with contingencies; one that is flexible and adaptable on both offense and defense. Remember, it is not your goal to predict the future. Your most important accomplishment will be a change in your business's attitude, mindset, or culture. In the end, creating an atmosphere for obtaining the "possible" could be your greatest strategic contribution.

2 Enhancing Greenhouse Profitability through Improved Marketing Planning

Charles Safely—North Carolina State University

Most business managers have heard the phrase, "Effective marketing is the key to profitability," but many do not fully understand what it means. The tendency is to associate marketing with "selling" or "advertising." These are, in fact, only a couple of aspects of marketing. From a managerial perspective, marketing may be defined as the total system of business activities designed to plan, price, promote, and distribute greenhouse products that satisfy the wants/needs of potential/present customers while achieving the business's objectives.

The major emphasis in this definition is the customer, first and foremost. The business that provides customers with what they want, when they want it, and how they want it will be the most successful. In an industry as large and diverse as the greenhouse industry, it is impossible to develop a general marketing program that would apply to all growers, because management skills, market opportunities, and resource availabilities vary considerably in each part of the country. Thus, step-by-step guidelines are presented here that can be used to develop an individualized marketing plan. The planning framework presented in this chapter (see figure 2.1 below) represents an application of the **strategic marketing planning process.** The process is practical, workable, and, with slight modification, can be used for any specific greenhouse operation. While developing a marketing plan alone cannot guarantee success, it does ensure that factors affecting the profitability and survivability of the greenhouse are considered.

Step 1
Analyze the Present Marketing Situation

The first step in the marketing planning process is analyzing the present marketing environment. Marketing objectives cannot be determined before an assessment is conducted of where the greenhouse presently stands in its total marketing environment. In conducting a

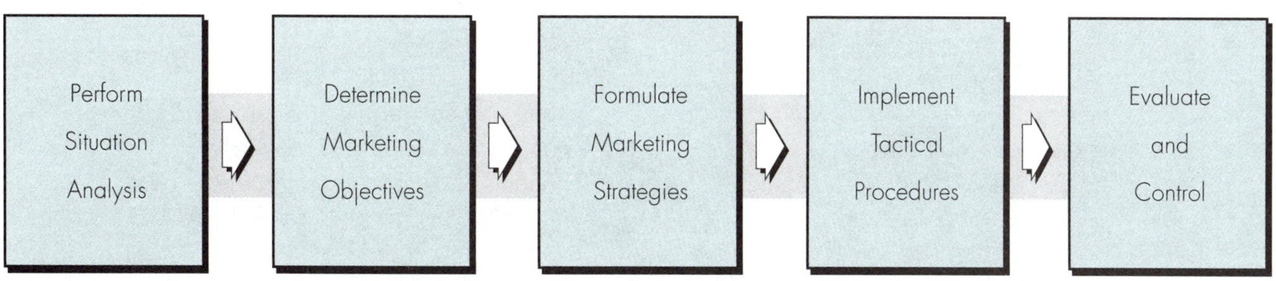

Figure 2.1. *The strategic marketing planning process*

situation analysis, the manager typically gathers two types of information: (1) internal or business-related information and (2) external or market-related information. Specific questions used to collect the appropriate information are presented in the sidebar below.

Sources of Information

- State or national trade associations
- Landscape contractors, retail buyers, and garden centers (can indicate plants they are currently using or plan to use and which ones are difficult to obtain)
- County extension agents and horticultural specialists (Cooperative Extension Service)
- State departments of agriculture
- Trade publications
- Trade shows
- Industry surveys
- Census data
- Internet
- Internal sources (own financial and production records, knowledge of employees, etc.)

INTERNAL AND EXTERNAL INFORMATION GATHERED IN THE SITUATION ANALYSIS

Business-Related (Internal) Information

(1) Financial resources and capabilities:

- Gross profits and net earnings after taxes
- Financial ratios—return on investment, breakeven analysis, leverage ratio, current ratio, age of accounts receivable, inventory turnover, working capital turnover, and profit margins
- Cash-flow analysis (actual and/or projected)
- Record-keeping system
- Borrowing capabilities

(2) Operating facilities:

- Production capacity—based on land, labor, and equipment availabilities
- Production scheduling of cultural practices
- Inventory levels by variety, grade, size, and loss rates (may affect markets targeted in the short run)
- Human resource requirements
- Equipment requirements

(3) Competitive strengths and weaknesses:

- Competitive status of company's products (name recognition, quality perception, etc.)
- Sales force capabilities
- Market share projections (as compared to competitors)
- Competitiveness of prices—volume discounts
- Advertising and promotion capabilities
- Depth of product mix
- Distribution methods and channels
- Service capabilities

Market-Related (External) Information

(1) Environmental constraints:

- Costs and availabilities of materials (chemicals, soil media, etc.)
- Costs and availabilities of energy (fuel, electricity, etc.)
- Economic conditions—housing starts, inflation, recession, interest rates, unemployment rates, capital availability
- Technology advancements
- Political environment—environmental quality, pesticide issues, etc.

(2) Market conditions:

- Market size—population, family size, number of households, rate of growth in an area, geographic concentrations
- Market segments differentiated by age, sex, income level, education, occupation, and other pyschographic variables
- Buyer purchasing habits—time, place, credit or cash, frequency
- Buyers' use habits—when, where, for what purpose

(3) Analysis of competitors:

- Number of competitors in the market area
- Market shares (industry surveys)
- Strengths and weaknesses in terms of prices (last three to five years), product mix, quality, promotion, advertising, cost structure, transportation costs

Target Market Selection

Once possible markets have been segmented, the next task is deciding which markets to target. This is based on the research findings and opportunities identified in the early stages of the situation analysis. Based on this segmentation, certain generic target market options exist for the firm:

1. Aim at the entire market (all segments) with a single marketing approach.
2. Pursue several different segments with different marketing approaches for each segment.
3. Focus on just one segment with a very direct marketing approach.

The old adage that marketing decisions should be based on marketing facts provides the foundation for situation analysis. In turn, the situation analysis provides a basis for establishing objectives and determining practical and realistic marketing strategies and tactics. One major point that needs to be emphasized here is that the situation analysis is an ongoing part of marketing planning. Its purpose is to keep the manager aware of changes taking place inside and outside the business. It should not be viewed as a one-shot or once-a-year activity.

Step 2
Determine the Marketing Objectives to Be Achieved

Objectives provide targets for the direction and guidance of the marketing plan. These objectives must be in line with the overall objectives of the greenhouse as well as with financial and production objectives. Marketing objectives are typically set in such areas as profit, return on investment, sales volume, market share, pricing, advertising, and promotion (see sidebar above). In determining marketing objectives, the manager should be guided by several criteria. Marketing objectives should be measurable, specific, consistent with overall business goals, attainable, and time-specific. The determination of realistic marketing objectives requires a sound situation analysis. Since these objectives will guide the entire plan and its strategies, they must be realistic and clear. However, they may need to be refined over time. Setting objectives is an ever-changing part of the planning process. As market situations and competition change, so must the marketing objectives.

EXAMPLES OF SPECIFIC MARKETING OBJECTIVES

- Increase overall return on investment by __% for the next fiscal year.
- Increase specific product sales by __% for the next fiscal year.
- Increase market share by __% in "X" market by December 31, 2XXX.
- Increase sales volume by __% in selected regions or territories by specific dates.
- Aim for prices that yield a minimum unit contribution to overhead of __%.
- Increase manpower training by __% by a specific date.
- Achieve advertising/promotion goals in specific markets for the year.
- Introduce __ new products to fill out product mix by specific dates.

Step 3
Formulate the Appropriate Marketing Strategies

At this point in the process, the manager's task is to determine an overall strategy to achieve the defined objectives. Four basic marketing strategies are (1) market penetration, (2) market development, (3) product development, and (4) diversification.

Using a market-penetration strategy, the greenhouse attempts to fill the needs of an existing market with its present product mix. This type of strategy may use a number of approaches. For example, the manager may wish to increase the number of customers in present markets or increase the usage of particular plants by both present and potential customers. In addition, the manager may also want to prevent competitors from taking away present customers.

A market-development strategy is one that attempts to find new markets for the greenhouse's existing product mix. The manager hopes to find new uses and/or new customers in new markets for plants that are already being produced and marketed. It is, of course, possible for any manager to employ market penetration and market development at the same time, since both involve the same product mix. Only the markets targeted are different.

A product-development strategy exists when the manager attempts to develop new products for customers in the business's present markets. A number of approaches may be used here as well. For example, a product improvement may be replacing an existing plant that is slipping in the marketplace with a new plant (cultivar). The new product may be less expensive to produce, more appealing, or more appropriate for the customer's landscaping or gardening needs. Maybe the business begins to offer current products in slightly different forms (plant size, combination pots, etc.). With this type of strategy, the manager wants to make a better impression in present markets through product changes and/or additions.

A diversification strategy occurs when the manager attempts to attract new groups of customers by moving into totally new markets with new products. This might involve taking a new product or service to totally new markets that the company didn't previously serve. For example, a logical diversification for some greenhouses may be adding outdoor nursery production, landscape contracting, or interiorscaping. With this approach, the manager hopes to move into markets not served with new products. Diversification is the most risky of the four strategies, because it involves departure from both the product and market experience of the firm.

Step 4
Establish Tactical Procedures for Implementing Strategy

After determining the overall strategy (or strategies), the next step in the planning process involves implementing and carrying out the strategies. This requires the development of marketing programs, which involve tactical elements. The marketing strategies must be transformed into a set of specific actions or tactics for accomplishing marketing goals. These tactics are often referred to as the marketing mix. Decisions concerning the marketing mix are presented in the sidebar on page 9. This list is not inclusive, nor do all decisions or activities pertain to every greenhouse manager. The marketing mix depends on which target markets are selected, the type of market strategy chosen, and requirements of customers as indicated in the situation analysis.

Step 5
Evaluate the Plan and Implement Control Procedures

Performance of the plan must be measured, and this means that standards must be developed against which performance can be evaluated. Typically, the manager develops quantitative measures of overall planning performance, such as the following:

- Comparing total sales and profits with figures from preceding years
- Measuring performance relative to competitors (i.e., market share)
- Performing a sales analysis by breaking down sales into categories, such as geographic region, primary customers, and fast-moving products
- Measuring customer satisfaction with surveys and other market feedback tools

The importance of proper and timely evaluation cannot be overlooked. Communication between the business and the customer is essential for success. Customers will try a new supplier "one time." If they are not pleased with the product, they will look elsewhere. A good evaluation system and prompt corrective actions, when required, can assist managers in maintaining their individual market share.

Properly conducted, this step allows the manager to evaluate what is right and wrong and to make corrective actions. This step forces the manager to consider how the results of each planning period's evaluation shall be used to improve performance in the next planning period. Information gained in the control-and-evaluation analysis may be used to update objectives, alter strategy approaches, and even change tactics to be used. When this happens, the planning process has come full circle, and the entire marketing planning process begins again.

DECISIONS CONCERNING THE MARKETING MIX

Product-Related Decisions

- Determining the most effective product mix (species, cultivars, sizes, etc.) to serve each market segment (should be based on costs and buyer demand)
- Branding the products in the product line, if possible (plant patents, etc.)
- Using attractive and efficient containers
- Providing attractive and informative labels for plant materials
- Providing guarantees for each product in the product line
- Modifying the existing product mix as the need arises
- Planning and introducing new products (cultivars, sizes, etc.) when possible
- Providing information on the care of the plants after they are sold
- Considering service options—delivery, credit, convenient business hours

Promotion-Related Decisions

- Selecting and prioritizing target groups and geographical marketing areas
- Determining whether advertising is required for the target markets selected; if so:
  - —Determining advertising appeals and specific messages to use in those campaigns
  - —Selecting appropriate advertising media, such as radio, television, newspapers, road signs, or direct mail
  - —Determining the size of the ads to be used
  - —Determining the duration of the advertising campaign
  - —Determining the frequency of advertising
  - —Determining how advertising effectiveness is to be measured
- Selecting appropriate sales promotional media, such as point-of-purchase materials, samples, demonstrations, or trade shows
- Developing a colorful, prominent logo
- Holding public-relations events—donate to charities, serve as a community meeting place, sponsor festivals, etc.

Pricing-Related Decisions

- Determining base prices for each grade of product in each market served
- Providing a certain profit margin
- Determining the appropriate types and sizes of volume discounts used, if any
- Determining the use of psychological pricing tactics, such as prestige pricing, promotional pricing, etc.
- Determining credit policies
- Allowing consumers to buy the quality of plants they can afford

Distribution-Related Decisions

- Providing protective packaging for goods in transit and storage
- Determining the modes of transportation to be used
- Determining inventory requirements and maintaining those requirements
- Providing frequent small shipments, even on weekends if necessary

3 Enhancing Greenhouse Profitability through Improved Personnel Management

Susan Barton—University of Delaware

The most important asset of an organization is the human asset, and the best measuring device for the quality of an organization is the quality of the people. Organizations with top-quality people are more profitable, because they have the most satisfied customers, the best company image, and the ability to weather economic slumps. Finding and keeping good employees is one of a manager's key tasks.

Labor is an important issue in the green industry. In fact, the labor situation was cited as the number one concern of surveyed greenhouse managers. Labor accounts for 26% of sales on average for the entire green industry and 28% of sales for the production segment of the industry. And the cost of labor is not just the salaries earned by employees. There are many additional hidden costs, such as Social Security, unemployment insurance, workers' compensation, and fringe benefits.

Managers consider cutting the labor budget as a way to reduce costs. This is usually a mistake. A better idea is to increase efficiency through careful hiring, effective training, motivational policies, and intelligent scheduling, which in turn will create a quality workforce that is the asset a company needs to be successful.

Often, employers don't put in as much time trying to find the right employee as they do worrying about the proper irrigation system. If growers spent more time thinking about their labor input, they could dramatically increase greenhouse performance.

Hiring/Selection

Set a goal for your company to "hire good employees and minimize mistakes." The cost of hiring and training a new person is staggering. The turnover that results from poor personnel management results in more money spent on training, recruitment, and selection; lost productive management time; lost business; and dissatisfied customers. Hiring decisions are so important that they are worth spending time on. Develop a planned set of steps for your hiring process:

1. Write job descriptions and position specifications.
2. Recruit a pool of candidates—advertise or otherwise search for candidates.
3. Prescreen for basic requirements/qualifications.
4. Develop a list of interview questions.
5. Interview.
6. Describe the company and give a timetable.
7. Check references.
8. Make a clear offer.
9. Provide new employee orientation and training.

Job Descriptions and Position Specifications

Job descriptions characterize a job and include the duties, responsibilities, and qualifications required to perform that job. Position specifications may characterize an ideal person and include the essential behavioral characteristics necessary for the job.

A position announcement should include the job title; the experience and education necessary to do the job; duties and responsibilities of the position; the position's place in the company hierarchy; paths for advancement; on-the-job training periods; and the position's stated purpose, such as "to monitor and control pests so plants can be produced efficiently and free from insects and disease." It may also include personality traits and characteristics considered desirable for the job. A position announcement that accurately describes the job will help potential employees determine whether they will be happy in the position.

Recruiting

The most frequently cited sources of new employees are employment agencies (specializing in the industry), high schools, trade schools, colleges, universities, classified ads, and current employees. Schools often offer a job-posting service. Attend career days at local universities to present information about your company. Or develop relationships with professors who teach greenhouse courses. You may be able to give a guest lecture about the industry and recruit employees at the same time.

Some schools have formalized internships and will help place students at willing businesses. Internships provide an opportunity to screen potential employees and offer positions to the best people. Some high schools have vo-tech programs that teach horticulture and greenhouse management. You may find eager students who are not college-bound but want the opportunity to grow with you.

Other businesses in the green industry are a great source of employees. Network with your suppliers and customers. Talk to people at trade shows. Place classified ads in industry trade publications. Use your "sphere of influence" to look for new employees wherever you go. Think about potential employees as you interact with people throughout the day. Carry business cards to solicit potential candidates.

Consider some nontraditional sources of employees. Part-time employees offer several advantages. They allow you to quickly expand the workforce to meet peak season/holiday workloads, but they rarely expect or receive benefits or overtime pay. Some employees with full-time jobs want to supplement their incomes with another part-time position. Other people who have caretaking responsibilities at home are not available for full-time employment but can meet a part-time schedule. Assign a manager the responsibility for scheduling part-time employees.

Disabled persons have been found to be more reliable, be more loyal, have less absenteeism, and remain in their positions longer than other types of employees. Also, there are tax benefits associated with hiring disabled employees.

Prescreening

Employment applications provide the first level of screening. Ask for the applicant's full name, address, and telephone number as well as information about the applicant's work experience, educational background, and specialized training. When requesting work experience data, ask for only the last three or four employers and leave room for employment periods, job titles, company names, addresses, phone numbers, and job duties. Ask applicants to write a statement (no less than 25 words) about their work and career goals. You can get an idea of how serious they are and an indication of their literacy. Some companies use a short screening interview, either in person or on the telephone.

Interviewing

A comprehensive interview enhances the company's image with the candidates and sets the tone for the rest of the work experience. When management spends time conducting thorough interviews, candidates understand the importance of personnel to the firm.

Prepare for the interview by developing a worksheet to record behavioral characteristics required for the job. Plan a set of questions designed to discover those characteristics. Look for absolute traits that are essential for the job. Consider behavioral traits that provide some insight into how the candidate will be motivated. Look at the interpersonal skills to discover how each person will work with the rest of your team.

Schedule a specific time and give the interview your full attention. Outline the procedure you plan to follow so the applicant knows what to expect. Verify the application information and ask a planned list of questions. Ask probing, open-ended questions that require more than a yes-no answer. Encourage the applicant to do most of the talking. Listen for statements that may indicate sincerity, goal orientation, enthusiasm, laziness, positive (or negative) attitudes, respect for co-workers and clients, and so on. Take notes and keep a record of the information you learn during the interview.

Use preemployment tests when appropriate. There are four general categories of preemployment tests—ability, skill-assessment, personality, and behavior tests. Ability tests reveal how quickly an applicant will learn your company's procedures and are the best predictor of job performance success. Skill-assessment tests provide an objective evaluation of an applicant's acquired skills. For example, if you need someone to perform a specific skilled task like pest scouting, test the applicant's skill level on a sample plant. Personality tests assign a value to various personality traits, such as assertiveness, extroversion, sensitivity, and efficiency. They often provide insight into how an employee can be motivated. Behavior tests measure whether an employee is likely to be reliable and productive.

If the applicant shows potential, give an overview of the company. Discuss the responsibilities of the position, to whom the person will report, the specific benefits and prerequisites, salary, working hours, and training. Avoid the temptation to hire an applicant on the spot. Provide a time frame within which you will notify the candidate.

Check references, especially former employers. Verify the information on the application and find out how the applicant interacted with fellow employees.

Selection

Don't let horticultural knowledge be the sole prerequisite for hiring. Good communications and organizational skills are also critical for many positions. Look for stability in work history with reasonable job changes. Always find out about missing times between jobs.

Use the completed worksheets and notes on each applicant to review potential candidates. Compare each applicant to a standard (the position specification) and not to one another. Discuss the candidates with at least one other member of the management staff. Avoid snap judgments, but don't ignore the "hunch" you feel about a potential candidate. Notify the candidate you've chosen, and conduct an expectation interview to review salary and benefits and to get a commitment from the candidate.

Legal Issues

Job applicants can file charges of discrimination if they can show that the gathering of even seemingly innocent information indirectly discriminates against them on the basis of sex, age, race, religion, handicap, or national origin. Avoid requests for the following information on applications and during the interview process:

- race, color, sex, religion, age, national origin, or citizenship
- age, birth certificate, or date of high school graduation
- height or weight
- a photograph
- future family plans, career path of spouse, or activities of the applicant's children
- club memberships
- arrest record
- criminal conviction, if not related to the position
- previous workers' compensation claims, or information about the applicant's past or present physical condition not related to work requirements
- an overseas residence or business

When hiring nonresidents, be careful to follow the letter of the law. It is up to the prospective employee to prove his or her identity and eligibility to work, but the business must request the person's credentials. Probationary periods can help you identify whether you have selected the right person for the job and give you an opportunity to correct your hiring mistakes by letting the wrong people go. Be sure to use quantitative guidelines during the probationary period to measure an employee's performance. You do not need a pre-established probationary period to evaluate a new employee's performance and discharge them if they are not meeting the standards you have outlined.

Training

Your behavior during the first day on the job will set the tone for the new employee's experience. One half hour of your time can mean the difference between a positive, upbeat beginning and a confusing, overwhelming one. Some employers try to spend a little time each day of the first week with new employees to offer coaching, encouragement, and guidance.

Employees need sufficient knowledge about a company's history, organization, key personnel, policies and procedures, products and services, market, and company niche. They also need to learn the key technical skills and people/communication skills required for the job.

Start by offering an orientation for new employees. Much of this information can be included in an employee handbook. An employee handbook provides an opportunity to clearly state what is expected from employees and what employees can expect from you. Employee handbooks make rules easier to enforce, since they apply to all workers. They also provide a level of protection against employee lawsuits. Include the following topics in an employee handbook:

- **Introduction**—include company history and philosophy
- **Hours**—outline normal and overtime expectations
- **Job attendance/tardiness**—define excused absences and repercussions of unexcused absences
- **Pay and salaries**—define method of determining pay
- **Benefits**—include paid vacations; health and dental insurance; sick leave; extended leaves for illness, pregnancy, or family matters; and retirement benefits
- **Drug and alcohol abuse**—outline policies regarding drug testing
- **Sexual harassment**—describe policy and outline steps for filing and handling claims
- **Discipline**—describe chain of events that will result from conduct that interferes with or adversely affects business
- **Employee safety**—stress importance and outline methods of reporting problems
- **Smoking**—establish policies consistent with state and local laws
- **Grievances**—outline filing procedure
- **Appearance**—outline dress code and grooming expectations
- **Termination**—include clause that reserves the right to terminate for any reason not stated in employee handbook

Schedule regular training sessions to communicate new product knowledge and teach technical and communication skills. Once you develop a schedule, stick to it. Continue training even during busy periods, just shorten the training time to 10, 15, or 30 minutes. Develop a notebook for each employee that documents training progress. Record new skills and competencies as they are learned.

People learn by example, repetition, reinforcement, and instruction. Break technical skills down into the primary components and address each one. Effective training sessions involve verbal and physical participation by employees. Help them retain information by letting them demonstrate new skills within the safety of a meeting. Use the following system to teach difficult technical skills:

1. You do and explain
2. You do while trainees explain
3. Trainees do and explain
4. Trainees do without explaining out loud

This system forces managers to think through how they complete a task so they are able to explain it clearly to employees. Role playing is a tool that works especially well with people/communication skills. Follow up training by assigning specific projects that integrate the skills you are teaching. Review the success, and change the training accordingly.

Design product-knowledge training sessions to focus on the benefits for the customer rather than a product's technical performance. Teach salespeople to listen to the customer's needs and present products that will meet those needs. Finally, use technical product features to substantiate the benefit claims.

Distinguish between behaviors and responsibilities. Responsibility is the desired outcome. For example, an employee might be responsible for keeping a poinsettia crop pest-free. The behavior necessary to complete that task might include posting yellow sticky cards, monitoring insect activity, and applying a particular pesticide with a backpack sprayer when insects reach the threshold for that crop. This definition of behavior clearly defines how management wants the employee to perform certain tasks. Training should include a description of how employees are actually supposed to do things. Include a time frame and materials required in the descriptions.

Evaluation

Conduct regularly scheduled performance evaluations. First, allow the employee to conduct a self-evaluation. Then schedule a performance review. Outline the procedure you will follow. Work from the job description for each employee. Specific job descriptions allow the manager and employee to work from the same checklist. This will determine whether behaviors are performed correctly or incorrectly, and evaluation will not be seen as a matter of opinion. Focus on observable, measurable components of a job that contribute to the organization's overall productivity and performance. Quality, quantity, timeliness, and cost are the four variables that can be measured and used to evaluate job performance.

When there is a problem with an employee, confront the issue. Often the employee does not realize what is happening. Explain how the problem affects business and discuss possible solutions. Get a commitment from the employee on a plan of action that will alleviate the problem. Employees are more likely to implement strategies they have developed and to which they have committed. At the end of the performance evaluation, agree on goals for the future. Document the discussion in each employee's file.

Managing and Leading

Motivation is not something you can do for (or to) a person. It must come from within. Employers can work to provide an environment in which employees want to work. To do this, identify the causes of high or low motivation, job satisfaction, and morale. Also learn how human needs affect motivation and morale. Common motivators include self-esteem; prestige and status; feeling of acceptance and belonging; recognition and appreciation by others; security and hope for the future; power and influence; reasonable independence and freedom of action; significant participation and involvement in activities affecting the company; and continuing growth and realization of potential through achievement, accomplishment, and contribution. Talk to your employees and find out about their personal goals. Develop a strategy that links those personal goals with goals of the company.

Compensation

Develop a pay structure that appropriately compensates employees for their contributions to the company and accurately reflects the resources of the company. Several industry trade journals conduct wage and salary surveys annually. Use these surveys to get an idea of the prevailing wage for different job categories in different regions of the country. Communicate the true compensation by reviewing the labor cost estimation worksheet with each employee (figure 3.1).

Hourly versus Salaried

There is a difference between hourly and salaried employees. A salaried employee is a "professional." He or she works as many hours as necessary "to get the job done." Extra hours on the job don't earn a salaried employee extra pay. On the other hand, salaried employees don't forfeit any pay for taking a few odd hours off for personal reasons. The commitment of extra time and effort when necessary presumably justified the professional's decision to use some time for personal purposes.

Federal law obligates employers to treat hourly wage earners differently from salaried workers. An hourly worker remains entitled to time-and-a-half for every hour worked beyond the 40-hour weekly standard. But the hourly worker also sacrifices income when his or her work week falls below the 40-hour standard. Unlike salaried workers, hourly workers sacrifice income if they take time from the workday for personal purposes.

Incentive Pay

Incentive pay can be used, in part, to motivate employees to do a specific task better or faster. To be successful, you must link incentive pay with performance over which employees have control. Start by establishing standards for piecework. Try to anticipate changes that will affect standards and loopholes that will reduce productivity. If quality is important, you can't reward quantity at the expense of a quality product. Involve employees in the development of an incentive-pay program. Make sure they feel comfortable that their pay won't decrease. Excite them about the opportunity to earn more. Provide feedback to employees by posting productivity numbers. Manage the system with a computer program that provides daily printouts on each worker's performance. List incentive pay separately on the weekly checks for positive reinforcement.

Some nurseries use vacation time as an incentive for non-full-time employees, measuring attendance and on-time arrival. This makes people think twice about

COST ITEM	COST TO *EMPLOYER*	INCOME TO *EMPLOYEE*
Direct wage costs:		
1. Total regular hours: ________ hours/week x ________ # weeks	= ________ hours	= ________ hours
Overtime hours: ________ hours/week x ________ # weeks	= ________ hours	= ________ hours
2. Cash wages (________ hours x ________ $/hour)	= $ ________	= $ ________
3. Overtime wages (________ hours x ________ $/hour)	= $ ________	= $ ________
4. Cash bonuses ($________ or ________ %)	= $ ________	= $ ________
5. **Total adjusted cash wages** (total lines 2 through 4)	= $ ________	= $ ________
Mandatory wage costs:		
6. Social Security (________ %)	= $ ________	= $ ________
7. Federal unemployment insurance	= $ ________	= $ ________
8. State unemployment insurance	= $ ________	= $ ________
9. Workers' compensation	= $ ________	= $ ________
10. Other	= $ ________	= $ ________
11. **Total value of mandatory costs** (total lines 6 through 10)	= $ ________	= $ ________
Value of fringe benefits:		
12. Insurance—life	= $ ________	= $ ________
health	= $ ________	= $ ________
dental	= $ ________	= $ ________
other	= $ ________	= $ ________
13. Retirement (firm's contribution)	= $ ________	= $ ________
14. Uniform (purchase/rental/cleaning)	= $ ________	= $ ________
15. Transportation (________ miles/day x ________ days x ________ $/mile)	= $ ________	= $ ________
16. Educational expense	= $ ________	= $ ________
17. Other	= $ ________	= $ ________
18. Other	= $ ________	= $ ________
19. **Total value of fringe benefits** (total lines 12 through 18)	= $ ________	= $ ________
20. **Total labor costs** (total lines 5, 11, and 19)	= $ ________	= $ ________
21. Hours paid but not worked (total)	= ________ hours	= ________ hours
holidays ________ hours		
vacation ________ hours		
sick leave ________ hours		
22. **Total hours on the job** (total line 1 and line 21)	= ________ hours	= ________ hours
23. Total costs per hour on the job (line 20 divided by line 22)	= $ ________	= $ ________

Figure 3.1. *Labor cost estimation worksheet*

missing work, and it rewards the people who deserve to be rewarded.

One greenhouse uses skill levels, character traits, and tenure to award incentive pay. They have developed two skill lists—one for production skills and one for retail skills. Each skill is rated according to its level of importance to the company and level of difficulty. Employees are rated on a scale of 1 to 10 on their level of proficiency at each task. A grade of 1 to 6 does not warrant compensation; however, a grade of 7 to 10 warrants varying extra hourly compensation. This system motivates employees to learn new skills.

The system also rewards desirable character traits like dependability, accuracy, and judgment. Compensation is raised based on evaluation of these traits. Quantifying these characteristics provides an opportunity to discuss sensitive issues. The third factor in the system is tenure with the company. Employees receive additional compensation for years of service after the second year. Experienced employees are valuable to the business and rewarded for staying.

Every employee is evaluated once a year by two managers and has an opportunity for self-evaluation. The scores are reviewed by the managers with the employee, and compensation is set for the following year.

Bonuses

Although even the most devoted employee will not work for pay that is substantially below what peers in the industry earn, salary increases are not the only way to reward productive employees. Reward excellent performance with bonuses, or offer an unscheduled holiday or increase in annual allowable vacation. Use praise to build trust and communicate that good performance is recognized and appreciated. To use praise effectively, be consistent with immediate and enthusiastic recognition whenever it is warranted. Be specific about which accomplishment you are acknowledging. Elaborate upon the benefits to the company that result from the employee's contribution.

Opportunities

Strive for high job satisfaction by allowing employees to organize their own work as much as possible. Structure jobs to provide variety and reduce boredom. Set goals with employees so they feel a sense of accomplishment and achievement. When career advancement is limited, offer employees the opportunity to cross-train and stimulate other interests through variety. Management and administrative positions are limited in a small business, but there are many other areas of responsibility that can enlarge and enrich a job.

Teambuilding

Build teams to improve communication, develop relationships, establish trust, and ultimately increase profits. An environment characterized by teamwork will be more receptive to customer demands.

Start by taking stock of the employees you have. List each employee's abilities and characteristics. Think about the role each might play in a team. Brainstorm about one or more new projects, and solicit input from all employees. Considering how employees express interest and your prior evaluations, assign them to work in teams on projects they have identified. Teams work best if you keep a scorecard to record team progress and increased productivity. Also, establish decision-making and conflict-resolution processes. Describe problems as opportunities to learn and continue to improve. Recognize employees who are working effectively, and provide immediate positive reinforcement. Celebrate when team goals are reached.

Termination

The current legal climate has made it difficult to fire an employee at will. The number of wrongful-discharge cases is increasing all the time. Even though most cases are settled out of court, the settlement and legal fees can be costly. To avoid unnecessary litigation, develop an employee-termination policy. Conduct regular employee evaluations and maintain records of the reviews. It is easier to discharge an employee with several written evaluations that document inadequate performance.

When you have to terminate an employee, make the termination interview as nonthreatening as possible. Assign the direct supervisor of an employee the task of conducting the termination interview. Avoid anger and personal attack.

Insurance

Workers' compensation is a significant expense for each employee. Workers' compensation laws and regulations vary from state to state. Consider implementing a self-insurance program, in which you save a specified amount per employee each pay period to cover potential claims. Couple the program with aggressive safety training to reduce on-the-job injuries. Create a climate that values safety.

Labor Efficiency

Two main issues affect labor efficiency. The first is individual efficiency or job performance, and the second is adjusting the supply of the various qualities of labor available to meet job requirements. Hire excellent people who are well suited to the assigned jobs. Motivate employees with a combination of pay incentives and work-environment adjustments. Train employees to help them reach their full potential. Then schedule employees efficiently by thoroughly understanding the needs of the business. Use the most significant asset of your company—your employees—to create a profitable and successful greenhouse business.

4 Enhancing Greenhouse Profitability through Product Mix Management

Bridget Behe—Michigan State University

Although cost analysis is the most basic information needed when considering which crops to grow, many other factors need to be considered. Turning inventory over into sales and profits will be critical to your business's success.

Examining the Customer Base

The first step is to consider your markets. A good understanding of who ultimately buys and enjoys the product you grow will help tremendously. Insight into customer desires helps you, and your customers, anticipate their demand. There is a growing trend among producers—small ones especially—to have a retail outlet of their own. In one *Season Sales Summary,** over 60% of small firms (with annual sales less than $250,000) had their own retail outlet compared to only 40% of large firms (with annual sales over $2 million). Having your own retail facility can give you a distinct advantage in your ability to monitor sales and customer preferences. This, in turn, can help you anticipate your production mix for the next year.

Differences among gardeners affect who buys which plants. Not all Americans garden for the same reasons. *Organic Gardening* magazine researchers identified four segments, or groups, of American gardeners: dabblers, cultivators, decorators, and masters.

* The *Season Sales Summary* was funded by **GM***PRO* magazine, along with the Ohio Florists' Association, and coordinated by Bridget Behe. The reports were discontinued after 2001 due to funding cuts.

Dabblers accounted for 61% of gardeners, but only 50% of sales. They spend only a few hours in the garden each week and likely would rather be playing golf or doing anything other than gardening. Since they spend so little time in the garden, they want to buy what they know or what will make them instantly successful. They are good candidates for the most familiar annuals and perennials. They will probably buy only red poinsettias and geraniums. They don't want to learn a lot about gardening but may slowly develop some new interests. They are apt to use container plants in bloom for instant gratification.

Cultivators accounted for 18% of gardeners and 17% of sales. These gardeners spend a few more hours each week in the garden but are mainly interested in vegetable gardening. They want to reap a harvest from the land. When marketing plants to them, the emphasis should be qualities of plants that are edible, not just ornamental. Any plants that are edible, including herbs, are good bets for them.

Decorators accounted for another 18% of gardeners, but 29% of sales. These gardeners are most interested in making their homes more beautiful. They coordinate flower color with home decor. They bring living space outdoors in decks and patios. They spend more time in the garden. They are most likely to buy nonred flowers and choose flowers that match a favorite color inside their homes.

Masters accounted for 3% of gardeners, but 4% of sales. They, like the decorators, are interested in something a bit different. Members of this group can be used as "opinion leaders" by giving them new plants to try in their gardens. They have lots of friends who ask them gardening questions. They can recommend your business and the new plants you've got. Recruit masters as marketing allies and get feedback from them frequently.

Gardeners don't all have the same interests or the same level of interest. Meet them where they are. Provide them with choices they'll see as appropriate. Don't push new plants on clients that want the old standbys, but be receptive to customers who are looking for something new and different.

Color preferences vary, and there are fashion trends in color. These trends are important for some gardeners. Most will buy what they know and stick to the basics. Less experienced gardeners probably prefer red flowers on green foliage, and they make up a great percentage of those who buy the top ten annuals. More experienced and appearance-conscious gardeners are likely looking for the hot "new" colors. How do you keep up with them? Look for "new" hot colors in fashion and home decor. Keep an eye on towels and sheets for a hint of what is next to be hot. It takes a few years for the color trends you see in fashion to make it outside to the garden.

Defining the Right Mix

After examining your customers, begin to think about specific plants to grow. Which annuals are you most likely to sell? If you have gardeners who are typical weekend gardeners, like the dabblers, your best bet for annual sales are the top twelve bestselling plants according to the *Season Sales Summary.* Each year, the *Season Sales Summary* reports the bestselling annuals and the top cultivar for each species. Recently, these included:

Impatiens—Super Elfin and Accent
Begonia—Cocktail
Geranium—Americana (cutting) and Pinto (seed)
Vinca—Cooler
New Guinea Impatiens —Paradise
Tomato—Better Boy
Pansy—Bingo
Dusty Miller—Silver Dust
Petunia—Wave, Madness, Ultra
Zinnia—Dreamland
Marigold—Bonanza
Snapdragon—Tahiti

Most gardeners will recognize these plants, although the cultivars might be new to them or they might not be aware of cultivars. If gardeners appear to be interested in color, introduce new cultivars to them by color. Most weekend gardeners won't be too interested in the new or more unusual plant, but some are. The more avid their interest, the more likely gardeners are to try something new. Anticipate this demand in your market. See how many want the top ten annuals, and see how many are looking for something new and different.

Consumers, retailers, and first producers are faced with an often overwhelming number of cultivar choices for any crop. There are over 30 red poinsettia cultivars on the market today, and an additional 30 pink, white, and novelty cultivars. Any seed catalog displays numerous petunia and pansy cultivars. The choices of mums can be even greater than poinsettias. Consider color preferences, crop timing, postharvest shipping characteristics, holding ability, and time to mature.

From the *Season Sales Summary,* we identified the top twelve bestselling perennials:

Echinacea 'Magnus'
Clematis x *jackmanii*
Rudbeckia 'Goldsturm'
Delphinium 'Magic Fountain'
Hosta 'Albo marginata'
Salvia 'May Night'
Coreopsis 'Moonbeam'
Astilbe 'Fanal'
Lantana 'New Gold'
Hemerocallis 'Stella d'Oro'
Verbena 'Homestead Purple'
Heuchera 'Palace Purple'

Most producers have seen perennials and know they are no longer "new" to plant production. With some customers, this is not true. Perennials aren't new to *some* gardeners, but they are new to *most* gardeners. Weekend gardeners might not be familiar with most perennials on the above list, even though they may have seen some at their local mass-merchandiser. They might think that all perennials are "low-maintenance" and need little attention. Perennials don't flower like annuals do; most show color for only a few weeks in the year, whereas annuals will have color for a few months of the year. Yet the perennials listed above are fun and relatively easy for most gardeners to grow. Experience is a good teacher, and these are easy perennials to get most gardeners started.

Determining Product Size

How do you know what size container in which to grow and market plants? Product sizes will vary with the retail outlet. There has been a trend in recent years for production to move to larger container sizes. Baskets are bigger, cell packs are bigger, even 4-inch pots are deeper than they were just a few years ago. Mass-merchandisers like large cell-pack sizes for bedding plants, because they don't need to be watered as often. Producers like them because they can make a bit more on each plant. Consumers appear to demand more mature "instant color" as the bedding-plant season progresses. Traditional "florist-grade" chrysanthemums and poinsettias are larger and have more flowers than many mass-market-quality plants. Before deciding on containers, survey your market. If it seems quite traditional, you should stay mostly with the container size consumers are used to seeing. It may take a while for them to change. However, you can try to introduce some larger containers that will bring higher prices and hopefully greater profits. Most markets are ready for this upgrade, but do it slowly.

Making a Production Plan

Now that you have narrowed the field of plants you want to grow and given some thought to container size, you are ready to make your production plan. The concept of square-foot-weeks helps you plan your inventory in the space and time available. Calculate how much space you have to determine production square footage. Then calculate how many weeks you need to grow the crop. The number of weeks multiplied by the amount of space gives you square-foot-weeks to finish that crop. If you have a greenhouse that measures 20 feet by 120 feet, you have 2,400 square feet each week to work with. It may be less if you have benches, so measure and see how much production space you have. For our example, we'll use 2,100 square feet of bench space each week for production.

If you want to finish flats that measure 12 inches by 18 inches, you need 1.5 square feet to finish them, spaced flat-to-flat. If you give each flat 3 square feet of space, you can finish 700 flats in this space. Or you can finish 2,100 6-inch poinsettias at a tight spacing (12 inches on-center) in the same area. If you spread them out to 18 inches on-center, you can finish only 933 poinsettias.

However, not all flats take the same amount of time. If you decide to grow all marigold flats to sell on May 15, you would have to sow them all eight weeks earlier. If you finish pansy flats from plugs, you may need only 12 weeks compared to 20 weeks if you grow them from seed. This is why plugs are sometimes an economical alternative for smaller growers, even though the cost is higher. When you account for losses in germination and the number of weeks you need to heat and grow pansies, you may be better off buying plugs.

Use square-foot-weeks as a tool to help you manage inventory and determine costs. Calculate how much growing space you have. You may choose not to count space overhead for baskets, even though they are there and growing.

Managing Inventory

An accurate crystal ball in the greenhouse industry is about as common as a blue rose. Weather in local markets is the single most critical variable in the marketability of greenhouse crops. A rainy, cold spring can ruin bedding-plant sales. A snowy Valentine's Day can be disastrous for delivery and plant material. A sunny Mother's Day weekend can sell out quickly. A warm fall can be welcome in cooler climates and bring in sales when none were expected. If you have it in color when the weather cooperates and the people want it and you have it at a competitive price, you probably can sell it.

It is hard to be prepared, but here are some things you can do if you're just getting started. Your main concerns will be temperature and rainfall. The first frost-free date is a good time to plant, and the last day before frost will give you an idea of the length of the growing season. Have tender plant material available two to four weeks before this date and hardy material four to six weeks before. You can find historical weather data for your markets on the Internet or from local sources. Ask your county extension staff about weather information. They will have some resources for you to use. Another great, readily available resource is the *Old Farmer's Almanac.*

If customers plant too early and lose purchases to a late spell of cold weather, you can capitalize on the replacements. But be aware that your professional advice may have spared the second purchase.

5 Enhancing Greenhouse Profitability through Improved Materials Handling and Distribution

Richard Harkess—Mississippi State University

Shipping and handling has been one of the areas of greatest need for improvement in labor savings. It is an area that has been improved little (Hammer 1998). Shipping is very labor- and time-intensive. Several aspects of shipping and handling can be addressed to improve profitability, including product movement in the greenhouse, the order-staging area, and packaging systems.

A greenhouse business cannot survive if its product does not make it to market. Your job is to either bring the market to you or move your product to the market. Bringing the market to the production site is the primary concern of retail greenhouse operations. Moving the product to the market is a primary concern of wholesale greenhouse operations. Whether selling retail out of your greenhouse or shipping to distant markets, your profitability will increase when the product arrives at market in the best possible condition.

Postharvest Quality

Increasing profitability may start with improving postharvest plant quality. Ethylene and temperature fluctuations during shipping often wreak havoc with plants. Choose cultivars that are known for their resistance to these factors. To determine appropriate cultivars, check with your seed supplier or read about the many trials that are conducted and published annually in the trade press. The industry has moved to larger container sizes to reduce the rapid drying of the cells on the retail shelf. There is a tradeoff to consider between greater shelf life and increased media costs.

Hardening-off plants by subjecting them to lower temperatures or withholding fertilizer or water can help extend shelf life. Cooling the plants before loading them onto delivery trucks will reduce excess respiration and transpiration during long-distance shipping, even when using refrigerated trucks. Temperatures in the trucks should be kept between 50° and 65°F, depending on the plant. In Michigan, one grower recommends shipping bedding plants at about 65°F, poinsettias around 62°F, and Easter lilies at 50°F, while a grower in Oklahoma recommends shipping most plants at 50°F early in the season and at 60°F late in the season to avoid too great a shock (Aylsworth 1997). Allowing the plant foliage to dry before loading can reduce humidity and the possibility of disease erupting during shipping. Maximizing ventilation or shipping in a refrigerated truck can reduce drastic temperature fluctuations during shipping. Make sure that the air circulation is not blocked, resulting in hot spots in the trailer. Clean the trucks between loads to reduce decaying plant debris, which can contribute to ethylene buildup (Davis 1998a).

Materials Handling Options

In a recent informal survey, growers were asked what changes have had the most impact on their businesses. Materials handling was among the most frequently mentioned areas for reduction of production costs

(Hammer 1998). An investment in concrete floors, walks, and driveways improves the effective use of materials-handling equipment. It is an investment that will save money in the long run.

Among the current most popular systems for materials handling is the use of metal shipping carts. These carts are useful throughout the greenhouse in every stage of production, from propagation to loading, shipping, and delivery.

Choosing a cart will depend on your needs and customer requirements. Determine your minimum aisle and door width and allow a 6-inch clearance for ease of maneuverability. Tire size, shelf material, and ability to collapse for storage are all factors to consider (McLean 1997, Socha 1997). Most manufacturers' carts have adjustable shelves. A cart with six shelves can carry as many as 42 10-inch-by-20-inch flats at a time. The carts are easily maneuverable, and most people have no problem handling several linked, fully loaded carts (Socha 1997). If you want to use carts but don't want to install concrete walks, then select carts with larger wheels that will move easily over gravel. Carts with tow bars can be linked and towed by an electric cart to quickly move a large volume of plant material through the greenhouse to the shipping staging area (Davis 1998b).

Carts offer several advantages in product handling. They are reusable, durable, and, with routine maintenance, long-lasting. Carts are better for shipping plants than hot, dark boxes (Socha 1997). [It should be noted, however, that some department stores still require everything to be boxed and palleted in spite of the advantages of carts.] Carts help keep the product fresher, because the plants spend less time on the truck. Loading efficiency is greatly increased. Loading that once took 20–30 hours can be done in two to three hours using carts. The carts have moveable shelves that allow great flexibility for plant height and help maximize the use of space. In addition, carts reduce the time required for making a delivery, and many retailers like to use them as display racks. When delivering a product to the retailer, it is easy to offload the loaded carts and load the empty carts from the retailer. Many designs and styles of carts are available. Collapsible carts offer an additional advantage in reduced space required for return shipping.

The disadvantages to using carts are the added inventory of the carts, maintenance, and damage and loss while at the retailer. Some wholesalers have reported that retailers will often use the carts for other companies' products. In these cases, the carts are often not empty for pickup and return. This can add to your cost by increasing the number of carts needed or by adding time at the retailer to wait while the carts are emptied. To combat this problem, some growers do not leave carts with the retailer.

Before investing in carts, consider the added expense of maintenance and storage. The carts require considerable space while waiting for loading on the shipping trucks, and space needs to be allotted for storage of empty carts. Regular maintenance is worth the expense to have the carts ready for the next season. Switching to carts should not be done halfway through the season. This can create problems with coordinating two shipping systems (Socha 1997).

Another reason for investing in carts is that they are synergistic with recent advances in bar coding. Many commercial greenhouse facilities have bar-coded carts. The code is read as carts are loaded and unloaded on trucks, thereby tracking carts and contents from producer to retailer and back.

PULLING ORDERS

Pulling orders can be one of the most time-consuming parts of shipping. Some growers have increased order-pulling efficiency by centralizing it. Order filling takes place in one location. The shipping room is lined with racks that have been filled with flats ready to ship. The racks are filled in the evening for the next day's shipping. In the busiest season, they are kept filled during the day as well. When an order is ready to be pulled, the order puller only needs to walk up and down the aisle pulling the required flats. This system has eliminated the need to run all over the greenhouse to fill orders. Each order, once pulled, is put on a cart or boxed for immediate shipment.

Distribution

There are several options in product distribution: owning your own trucks, contracting truck services, joining or forming a cooperative, or relying on commercial shipping operations. Your product, market, and size of operation will help determine the best method of product distribution.

If your market is primarily within one-half to one day's drive of your operation, owning your trucks may be a feasible means of product distribution. The costs of maintenance, depreciation, insurance, equipment replacement, driver salaries, and market distribution need to be considered. If your market is spread over a large geographic area with sparsely located customers, the costs in mileage and driver time may be prohibitive. The advantages to owning your own trucks include control over product handling during shipping, and customer contact. In addition, if you are working under a guaranteed sales contract, it allows you to pick up unsold product to be returned.

If you need additional trucks during the peak growing season, consider leasing rather than buying them, as they may sit idle during slower times of the year. By leasing, you will avoid the added costs of maintenance, repair, insurance, and vehicle registration (Davis 1998b).

Contracting with a trucking company to distribute your product is another means of getting your product to market without owning your own trucks. This type of arrangement can be very effective as long as the trucking company is informed about the required conditions for hauling your product. The biggest disadvantage is putting your crop in the hands of people who may not be trained to handle plants. This may lead to reduced crop quality as a result of shipping conditions.

Cooperatives centered on product marketing and distribution are an important means of getting the product to the customer in several countries. Usually the grower will enter into an agreement with the cooperative to sell either a specified percentage or all of their product through the cooperative sales office. The cooperative may provide a distribution network, which includes picking up the crop from your greenhouse and then distributing it with other growers' crops to the customer. In order for a cooperative of this type to work effectively, there must be a concentration of growers within a relatively small area to minimize distance to the distribution center. In joining a cooperative, the grower may have to give up some independence concerning what crops and how many are grown. There is also little grower recognition by the customer. The advantages to joining a cooperative include a reduced marketing staff, no need to purchase equipment or trucks, and an increased market through better distribution (growers can buy items with cooperatives at reduced prices). A cooperative, in gathering crops from several growers, can act as a rewholesaler and offer its customers a wider range of product than is available from an independent grower. By joining a cooperative, it may be possible to reach customers you could not afford to sell to before, because the volume needed by the customer was too small.

An alternative to forming or joining a cooperative is to make use of cooperative shipping. In 1990 in Oregon, a system was devised in coordination with area truck brokers to allow growers to ship small orders for a reasonable price by combining orders with other growers on the same trailer (Cuny 1997). With this type of system, shipping prices are controlled by pooling orders with similar destinations. Each grower is charged with his or her portion of the load and final destination.

Freight charges are usually calculated by including mileage, weight, dollar value, and volume (Ooykaas 1998). One greenhouse came up with an equation to use in an attempt to help nurseries determine total freight and drop charges. This formula has been pro-

ADVANTAGES OF USING COMPUTERS

Computers are quickly becoming an important tool in organizing shipping. Software packages exist that automate ordering, order pulling, and shipping routes (Davis 1998b, Hopkins 1998). Shipping software can reduce shipping costs 10–20% by allowing managers to get a better handle on per-mile costs, wage costs, and drop costs. Some systems can track production schedules and track billing, ordering, and labor expenses. Integrated with mapping software, the plant inventory-control and accounting software can map delivery points, distances, and plant material needed for each stop (Davis 1998b). The computer will generate shipping lists for each delivery, including the delivery route, mileage, and order lists. Workers are told by the computer what plants to pull for shipping and how to arrange the orders in the shipping area for each delivery route. Computers are becoming increasingly indispensable for production scheduling, calculating costs, and inventory control.

posed as an equitable method of splitting shipping costs on combined orders. The equation uses only mileage and volume factors to evenly divide shipping costs among the nurseries receiving deliveries. Charges are calculated by first taking the total mileage from the point of origin to the final destination and dividing each customer's distance from the origin by that number. This results in a percentage of the mileage the load is carried. Next, add that number to the percentage of the load for each respective customer. Finally, divide that number by 2 to arrive at the percentage of the total freight and drop charges to bill each customer. This equation can help determine shipping costs for split orders from a common ship point.

Depending on the product and the quantity to be shipped, commercial package-delivery or air-freight companies may be a feasible means of product distribution. Plugs, liners, and cuttings are often shipped using these companies. Many of these companies specialize in quick delivery times, which can reduce product damage due to shipping. Using a package-delivery company once again takes the product handling out of the grower's control. They are also not feasible if shipping large plants that are easily damaged by rough handling.

6 Enhancing Greenhouse Profitability through Improved Equipment Purchasing

Robin Brumfield—Rutgers University

The greenhouse industry has become a mature industry after many years of phenomenal growth per year. In a growth market, producers can produce a good product and find a market for it and be fairly sure of making a profit. In a mature market, competition is more intense and managers must focus on cost controls to stay competitive. Success in the greenhouse business requires both technical and business management skills. Greenhouse managers who are evaluating whether or not to adopt new technical aspects of the greenhouse must consider impacts not only on efficiency but also on the bottom line. Since labor is the highest cost in most greenhouses, representing 35–40% of sales, many managers are considering purchasing labor-saving equipment such as flat fillers and transplanters. A major goal of greenhouse managers should be to maximize the firm's profits. Thus, managers must determine what the purchase of new equipment will do to the bottom line.

Evaluating Strategic Alternatives

Once alternative production strategies have been selected, they need to be evaluated. This is the stage at which you will want to do some kind of financial analysis. You will want to follow three basic investment criteria:

- Larger benefits are preferred to smaller ones.
- Early benefits are preferred to later ones. This takes into account the time value of money—i.e., a dollar today is worth more than a dollar tomorrow.
- Safety is preferred to risk.

In addition to financial analysis, you will also want to analyze how these alternatives address the firm's other objectives. Some items to consider are:

- Which alternative will best enable the firm to reach its desired objectives?
- Which alternative best matches the firm's skills and resources (financial, technical, personnel, etc.)?
- Which alternative best meets management's personal preferences or sense of social responsibility?
- Which alternative minimizes the creation of new problems?
- What other activities am I involved in now, and how will each alternative affect those?
- How much time will be required to incorporate each alternative efficiently?

Don't forget to include the employees in the planning and evaluation process. Employees are often closer to problems than owners or managers. They often can contribute to recommendations and solutions to problems. Knowing that their opinion is valued also can improve their job satisfaction and productivity.

Selecting a Basic Strategy

Selection of the final strategy may involve tradeoffs among various objectives. One alternative may offer the greatest financial returns, but it may be inconsistent with other objectives. At this point, the manager must make a decision as to which objectives are most important.

Using Quantitative Tools to Aid in Planning

American businesses are using more sophisticated techniques in planning than ever before. The increased power of computers is making these techniques available for small businesses as well. Specialized analytical programs will continue to be developed for the greenhouse industry to help analyze alternatives. We will look at two alternatives as an example here. We will assume a greenhouse that produces 50,000 bedding-plant flats per year. The greenhouse is considering buying either a small flat filler that costs $6,900 and should last ten years or a transplanter that costs $35,000, lasts ten years, and can transplant 9,000 plugs per hour.

To make some comparisons, let's assume that labor costs $8 per hour, including the employer's cost of benefits. With manual labor, it takes one minute to fill a flat and three minutes to transplant a flat with 36 plugs. The flat filler can fill eight flats per minute and requires two employees, one to feed the flats and one to take them to the greenhouse. The transplanter requires five people: one to feed plug flats, one to fix flats that the machine misses, and three to move the flats from the transplanter and take them to the greenhouse. Thus, the labor savings are as follows.

Flat filler:

Manual labor for 50,000 flats @ 1 flat/minute and $8 per hour	$6,666.67
Flat filler for 50,000 flats @ 8 flats/minute and 2 people at $8 per hour each	$1,666.67
Difference is 833 total hours manually versus 208 hours using a flat filler	$5,000.00

The manual system requires four times as much labor.

Transplanter:

Manual labor for 50,000 flats @ 3 minutes/flat and $8 per hour	$20,000.00
Transplanter for 50,000 flats @ 9,000 plugs/hour, 36 plugs per flat, and 5 people at $8 per hour each	$ 8,000.00
Difference is 20 flats/hour/person manually versus 50 flats/hour/person using a transplanter	$12,000.00

The manual system requires 2.5 times as much labor.

Intuition

The technique most commonly used by greenhouse owners in the past is intuition. Good management is part science and part art, so intuition should not be discounted. However, a more sound plan will probably be developed by combining intuition with a more quantitative method to measure the potential returns.

Payback Method

After intuition, the payback method is probably the most common method used by greenhouse owners and managers in making investment decisions. In this method, the manager determines how soon a proposed investment will pay for itself, "the payback." Our flat-filler example requires an initial invest of $6,900 and saves $5,000 per year in labor costs, so it will have a payback of 1.4 years (in table 6.1, $6,900 ÷ $5,000 = 1.4 years). Managers who use this method generally set a maximum length for the payback period and reject investment alternatives that exceed the maximum payback period. Of several alternatives, they choose the one with the shortest payback.

While the payback method is simple and easy to use, it has some serious limitations. It does not take into account the size of the return. For example, our transplanter costs $35,000 initially and saves $12,000 per year in labor costs. Its payback is 2.9 years (in table 6.1, $35,000 ÷ 12,000 = 2.9 years). Therefore, the manager would chose the flat filler instead of the transplanter. However, both systems are expected to last for ten years, and over the ten-year period, the transplanter yields higher returns. The payback method ignores the benefits occurring in the years after the payback period.

Another drawback of the payback method is that it ignores the time value of money. For example, it gives equal weight to $1 received in year one and year two. But $1 received in year one could be invested and will be worth more than $1 received in year two.

— TABLE 6.1 —

ANALYSIS OF INVESTING IN A FLAT FILLER OR TRANSPLANTER USING THE PAYBACK METHOD

Year	*Flat filler*	*Transplanter*
0	(6,900)	(35,000)
1	$5,000	$12,000
2	$5,000	$12,000
3	$5,000	$12,000
4	$5,000	$12,000
5	$5,000	$12,000
6	$5,000	$12,000
7	$5,000	$12,000
8	$5,000	$12,000
9	$5,000	$12,000
10	$5,000	$12,000
Total benefits	$43,100	$85,000
Payback years	1.4	2.9

Net Present Value

The net present value method uses the time value of money. The net present value of an investment alternative is simply the difference between the present value of the benefits and the present value of the costs. If the net present value is positive, the financial answer is to invest, or to choose the alternative with the highest net present value.

To take into account the time value of money in investment decisions, all costs and returns are discounted so that they are expressed in today's dollars. Discounting is merely the reverse of compounding. Compounding tells how much a present dollar will be worth in the future. The future value of $1 equals the present value times the compound interest rate. The formula is:

$$FV = PV \times (1 + i)^n \text{ where:}$$

FV = Future value   i = Interest rate
PV = Present value   n = Number of years

Thus, at a 5% interest rate,

$$FV = \$1 \times (1+.05)^1 = \$1.05$$

To find the present value, we just rearrange the formula to solve for PV:

$$\frac{FV}{(1+i)^n} = PV$$

In this case, the "i" represents the discount rate, or the rate used to discount future dollars to represent their present value, or value today. The discount rate can be thought of as the interest rate plus a risk factor. Currently, certificates of deposit are totally risk-free and range from about 3.5% to 5% depending on how long you agree to tie up your money. So you may want to chose an interest rate of 3–5% and add 2–3% to reflect the riskiness of growing and marketing greenhouse crops. A more simplified formula is:

$$PV = d \times FV$$

Here, "d" equals the present value factor, which represents the value of $1 to be received at the end of the designated year and discount rate from table 6.2 (page 28). You can see that $1 received 20 years from now is worth only $0.06 in today's dollars with a discount rate of 15%. With computer programs, we do not need to do all of these calculations; the computer will do them for us. This allows us to take into account other factors such as depreciation and income tax. At an income tax rate of 15%, and using the seven-year declining balance method, we can calculate the net present value of investing in the flat filler and transplanter.

The net present value is the sum of the present values for each year minus the initial investment cost. In the example given earlier, using a discount rate of 8%, the net present value of the transplanter is greater than the net present value of the flat filler (tables 6.3 and 6.4, page 28). The flat filler would be chosen based on the payback method. But the net present value method takes into account the time value of money, the relative sizes of the net present values, and the costs and returns for the entire length of the investment—including those after the payback period. The one drawback to the net present value method is that it is only as accurate as the discount rate chosen. Since both items have a positive net present value, both should be purchased if funds are available under the assumptions in this example.

— TABLE 6.2 —

PRESENT VALUE OF $1.00 TO BE RECEIVED AT END OF YEAR INDICATED AT VARIOUS INTEREST RATES

Year	5%	6%	7%	8%	9%	10%	11%	12%	13%	14%	15%
1	.952	.943	.935	.926	.917	.909	.901	.893	.885	.877	.870
2	.907	.890	.873	.857	.842	.826	.812	.797	.783	.769	.756
3	.864	.840	.816	.794	.772	.751	.731	.712	.693	.675	.658
4	.823	.792	.763	.735	.708	.683	.659	.636	.613	.592	.525
5	.784	.747	.713	.681	.650	.621	.593	.567	.543	.519	.497
6	.746	.705	.666	.630	.596	.564	.535	.507	.480	.456	.432
7	.711	.665	.623	.583	.547	.513	.482	.452	.425	.400	.376
8	.677	.627	.582	.540	.502	.467	.434	.404	.376	.351	.327
9	.645	.592	.544	.500	.460	.424	.391	.361	.333	.308	.284
10	.614	.558	.508	.463	.422	.386	.352	.322	.295	.270	.247
11	.585	.527	.475	.429	.388	.350	.317	.287	.261	.237	.215
12	.557	.497	.444	.397	.356	.319	.286	.257	.231	.208	.187
13	.530	.469	.415	.368	.326	.290	.258	.229	.204	.182	.163
14	.505	.442	.388	.340	.299	.263	.232	.205	.181	.160	.141
15	.481	.417	.362	.315	.275	.239	.209	.183	.160	.140	.123
16	.458	.394	.339	.292	.252	.218	.188	.163	.142	.123	.107
17	.436	.371	.317	.270	.231	.198	.170	.146	.125	.108	.094
18	.416	.350	.296	.250	.212	.180	.153	.130	.111	.095	.081
19	.396	.331	.277	.232	.194	.164	.138	.116	.098	.083	.070
20	.377	.312	.258	.215	.178	.149	.124	.104	.087	.073	.061

— TABLE 6.3 —

NET PRESENT VALUE ANALYSIS OF PURCHASING A SMALL FLAT FILLER FOR $6,900 DISCOUNTED AT 8% AND AN INCOME TAX RATE OF 15%

Year	Item	Outlay and depreciation	Effect after income tax (15%)	Reduced labor costs	Income tax effect (1–.15=.85)	Annual amount
0	Initial outlay	$ 6,900	$ (6,900)			$ (6,900)
1	Depreciation tax shield (10.71%)	$ 739	$ 111	$ 5,000	$ 4,250	$ 4,361
2	Depreciation tax shield (19.13%)	$ 1,320	$ 198	$ 5,000	$ 4,250	$ 4,448
3	Depreciation tax shield (15.03%)	$ 1,037	$ 156	$ 5,000	$ 4,250	$ 4,406
4	Depreciation tax shield (12.25%)	$ 845	$ 127	$ 5,000	$ 4,250	$ 4,377
5	Depreciation tax shield (12.25%)	$ 845	$ 127	$ 5,000	$ 4,250	$ 4,377
6	Depreciation tax shield (12.25%)	$ 845	$ 127	$ 5,000	$ 4,250	$ 4,377
7	Depreciation tax shield (12.25%)	$ 845	$ 127	$ 5,000	$ 4,250	$ 4,377
8	Depreciation tax shield (6.13%)	$ 423	$ 63	$ 5,000	$ 4,250	$ 4,313
9				$ 5,000	$ 4,250	$ 4,250
10				$ 5,000	$ 4,250	$ 4,250
	Net present value, 8% discount rate					$ 22,381

— TABLE 6.4 —

NET PRESENT VALUE ANALYSIS OF PURCHASING A SMALL TRANSPLANTER FOR $35,000 DISCOUNTED AT 8% AND AN INCOME TAX RATE OF 15%

Year	Item	Outlay and depreciation	Effect after income tax	Reduced labor costs	Income tax effect (85%)	Annual amount
0	Initial outlay	$ 35,000	$ (35,000)			$(35,000)
1	Depreciation tax shield (10.71%)	$ 3,749	$ 562	$ 12,000	$ 10,200	$ 10,762
2	Depreciation tax shield (19.13%)	$ 6,696	$ 1,004	$ 12,000	$ 10,200	$ 11,204
3	Depreciation tax shield (15.03%)	$ 5,261	$ 789	$ 12,000	$ 10,200	$ 10,989
4	Depreciation tax shield (12.25%)	$ 4,288	$ 643	$ 12,000	$ 10,200	$ 10,843
5	Depreciation tax shield (12.25%)	$ 4,288	$ 643	$ 12,000	$ 10,200	$ 10,843
6	Depreciation tax shield (12.25%)	$ 4,288	$ 643	$ 12,000	$ 10,200	$ 10,843
7	Depreciation tax shield (12.25%)	$ 4,288	$ 643	$ 12,000	$ 10,200	$ 10,843
8	Depreciation tax shield (6.13%)	$ 2,146	$ 322	$ 12,000	$ 10,200	$ 10,522
9				$ 12,000	$ 10,200	$ 10,200
10				$ 12,000	$ 10,200	$ 10,200
	Net present value, 8% discount rate					$ 37,316

Internal Rate of Return

The internal rate of return is the rate at which the net present value of the benefits is equal to cost. Rather than use a predetermined discount rate as with the net present value method, the internal rate of return method uses the same formula as the net present value method and solves for the discount rate. You chose the investment with the highest discount rate or internal rate of return. This is a very long process to do by hand, but spreadsheet programs now have functions that allow you to solve for the discount rate. In the example we used earlier, the discount rate is 63% for the flat filler and 29% for the transplanter. Therefore, the flat filler would be chosen using the internal rate of return method, whereas the transplanter would be chosen using the net present value method. One problem with the internal rate of return method is that it does not take into account the size of the return. An investment with a high internal rate of return but low return in terms of dollars of profit would be chosen over an alternative with a lower internal rate of return but a higher net present value. Again, since both investments have very high internal rates of return, both are good investments if funds are available.

In Conclusion

Several tools are available to determine the profitability of alternative systems and investments in labor-saving technology. This chapter describes the process one should use in determining how to evaluate alternative systems from a financial and management prospective. However, profits may not be the only objective of the business. The manager must determine whether the system is consistent with the strategic plan. If it is not, should it be rejected, or should the strategic plan be reevaluated? Do you have many crops, making automation less efficient than in the examples presented in this chapter? How efficient is your labor? Make sure your own analysis reflects how many flats you produce and your discount rate, tax rate, and wage rate, and includes any other factors that need to be considered. The investment decision will vary depending on these factors.

7 Enhancing Greenhouse Profitability through Improved Cost Accounting

Robin Brumfield—Rutgers University

Every day in the life of the greenhouse manager is filled with the monumental task of making decisions. Some of these decisions are general. Is the operation profitable enough to ensure survivability for the next five or ten years or longer? Am I marketing a quality product at a price that is competitive with industry prices? Does my business have a reputation of being honest, fair, and considerate of the customer?

Other decisions tend to be more detailed. What size plants should I grow? Should I invest in new machinery or technology? What price should I try to negotiate for this item? What product mix will yield the highest profit? Should I produce my own plugs, buy them from someone else, or use a conventional seeding system? How many plugs should I put in each pot?

The primary responsibility of any greenhouse manager is to make decisions that will answer these types of questions and achieve the objectives of the firm. And, of course, maximizing profits is generally one of the most important objectives of any operation. But managers are faced not only with making decisions that potentially affect revenues and costs of the firm, they must also implement solutions in a manner that is both efficient and effective.

Cost accounting or budgeting is a tool that may be used to help make these decisions. In general terms, cost accounting or budgeting can be defined as a plan to allocate resources among alternative uses. These resources include labor, water, capital, and any other resources that may be scarce or limited. Budgets can also be used to provide a basis for planning labor needs and for financing (such as deciding when to borrow and how much). They also provide a plan for when to buy supplies and when to sell your products.

Cost-accounting budgets are especially effective when a record system designed for managing is already in place. Records are especially important in that they provide feedback for evaluating performance and provide information for developing and refining budgets. Thus, the effectiveness of budgeting is a function of how good your record-keeping system is. Tax records are the most common type of records kept by greenhouse managers. They provide a good picture of the costs and returns of your entire business from a tax-accounting standpoint. However, most producers grow numerous crops, and tax records will not provide information on the costs and returns from any individual crop. Only through cost accounting can you allocate the costs involved in operating your business to specific crops.

Though cost accounting and record keeping are valuable managerial tools, they require time to maintain and therefore represent a cost themselves. The costs of preparing and maintaining budgets and records must be included in the total cost of the business. These items aid the manager in making sound management decisions, so the benefits certainly outweigh any costs involved.

As an example of cost accounting—information regarding the production of geraniums from unrooted cuttings—is included in table 7.1. Figures in the table represent updated information originally reported by Brumfield in *Tips in Growing Zonal Geraniums.* It was assumed in this analysis that one cutting per 4-inch pot was used at a cost of $0.14 per cutting and that the geraniums took 13 weeks to finish.

Costs are generally categorized into fixed (overhead) and variable costs. Variable costs are attributed to the production of a specific crop and increase as the number of plants produced increases (and vice versa). Fixed or overhead costs do not vary directly with the production of a specific crop. They remain constant regardless of level of output and are incurred even if production does not take place.

Variable Costs

Variable costs are estimated by multiplying the quantities of each input used by their input prices. They can be determined easily from invoices but may have to be allocated to the appropriate crop. Materials should be charged directly to each crop according to the amount used. It is a little more difficult to allocate the costs of labor, machinery, and equipment to any one crop. That is where detailed records really pay off. They greatly simplify this allocation process.

Material costs are the easiest variable costs to allocate. These include the costs of cuttings, pots, growing medium, fertilizer, and other chemicals. Costs of individual inputs will vary from producer to producer, depending on quantity discounts, method of payment, rate of fertilization, pesticide practices, and other managerial decisions. Materials costs per 4-inch geranium in the example totaled $0.26, as shown in table 7.1.

Production labor is slightly more difficult to allocate to each unit, but with some simple record keeping, it can be accomplished. Many of these tasks are done for one size container over a period of several hours. Simply note the number of people performing the operation and when they start and finish. Then count the number of units they finish in that time period. From this, you can calculate the time per unit and multiply it by the wage rate, including benefits. This will give you the cost of that specific labor task per unit. This method is not exactly precise, but you will be amazed at how consistent the time per flat will be if you time the operation on several different days. Once you time an operation, you can use that time frame in your cost accounting with a good deal of confidence. Of course, you will always have some unallocated labor (trips to and from the greenhouse, breaks, etc.), which can be included in overhead costs and allocated on a per-square-foot-week basis.

— TABLE 7.1 —

COSTS OF PRODUCING GERANIUMS GROWN IN 4-INCH POTS FROM UNROOTED CUTTINGS

Variable costs	*$ per pot*
Materials	
Unrooted cutting	$0.14
Oasis cube	$0.02
4-inch plastic pot	$0.05
Fertilizer	$0.01
Growing media	$0.03
Chemicals	$0.01
Labor	$0.13
Interest on operating capital	$0.02
Subtotal of variable costs	**$0.41**
Overhead costs	*$ per square foot per week*
Depreciation	$0.025
Insurance	$0.005
Repairs	$0.006
Taxes	$0.001
Interest on fixed assets	$0.024
General overhead items	$0.021
Subtotal of overhead costs	**$0.082**
13 weeks x .25 square foot per pot x $0.082 per square foot per week =	$0.27
Total costs per 4-inch geranium	**$0.68**

Note: It was assumed in this analysis that one cutting per 4-inch pot was used at a cost of $0.14 per cutting and that the geraniums took 13 weeks to finish.

Remember: These are not your costs! This example is provided only to illustrate a method of determining costs that apply to your operation.

Production labor costs for this example were estimated using a wage rate of $6.45 per hour. The total amount of labor needed to produce one 4-inch geranium was 73.60 seconds (15 seconds to stick the cutting, 15.50 seconds to pot the cutting, 4.80 seconds to apply pesticides, 14.60 seconds to water and fertilize, and 23.70 seconds to harvest). Thus, the production labor charge totaled $0.13 per 4-inch geranium.

Interest on the amount of money it takes to cover materials and production labor costs must also be accounted for. First, determine the annual interest rate and divide by 52 to obtain the weekly interest rate. Next, multiply that figure by the number of weeks your money will have been used from the time production costs are first incurred until the 4-inch geraniums are sold. The interest rate is assumed to be 12% for this example.

Overhead Costs

Overhead costs include depreciation, interest on fixed assets, repairs, taxes, insurance, and general categories such as managerial salaries, utilities, office expenses, professional fees, advertising and promotional expenses, and bad debts. These costs cannot be allocated to specific crops but can be allocated on some other basis, such as cost per square-foot-week. To do this, take all overhead costs and divide by the number of weeks in production to obtain an annual overhead cost per week. Next divide that number by the actual square footage of greenhouse bench space to determine the overhead costs on a per-square-foot-week basis.

Overhead costs for a typical unheated 100,000-square-foot greenhouse operation are estimated to be about $0.082 per square-foot-week ($0.025 for depreciation, $0.005 for insurance, $0.006 for repairs, $0.001 for taxes, $0.024 for interest, and $0.021 for general overhead items). For greenhouses that are heated, typical overhead costs may range up to $0.20 per square foot per week. In this example, the overhead cost per 4-inch geranium may be calculated as follows: 13 weeks in production × $0.082/square foot/week × 0.25 square foot/plant = $0.27/plant

Total Costs

As seen in table 7.1 (page 31), total costs for producing a 4-inch geranium are $0.68 per plant. This assumes an ideal situation where all the geraniums produced are saleable. Unfortunately, in reality, this is not the case. Some plants are lost to insects, diseases, or cultural problems, while others may be of such poor quality that they just cannot be sold. When losses occur, the empty bed space increases overhead costs per week, in addition to the variable costs that are lost. These types of factors must be considered when determining the true costs of production.

Uses of Cost-Accounting Information

Now that we've discussed how cost accounting budgets are developed, let's talk about how they can be used. First of all, the estimated profit of various crops can be compared to select the more profitable crops and crop combinations. You may be producing crops that are not breaking even, which is not a very competitive situation to be in.

By the way, breaking even in cost-accounting terms is not necessarily a bad thing. Remember that all costs are being covered, including opportunity costs. Positive expected profits may be viewed as a return to risk or entrepreneurial talents.

One of the most important uses of cost-accounting budgets is helping to establish a minimum selling price based on production costs. There are many different ways of pricing horticultural products—some are good and some not so good. Probably one of the most common pricing methods is to check what your competitors are charging for similar products and charge about the same price for yours. However, if you do this, you are assuming that (1) your competitors know their production costs and are pricing their products to cover those costs and (2) your production costs are the same or less than your competitors. If either of these assumptions is incorrect, the possibility of losing money exists.

Another popular pricing strategy is to increase prices on all products a given percentage every year or so. This strategy assumes that any changes in costs of production affect all enterprises similarly, which is simply not true.

The best pricing strategy considers the value customers place on your product. However, cost-accounting procedures can help you know the base minimum price you should charge for your product to cover all costs. The final selling price you charge ultimately depends on the value you feel your customers place on your product, which should include a fair return on your investment and the risks associated with producing greenhouse crops. By using costs of production as a guide, you are at least guaranteeing that all of your costs are covered and that you are not producing unprofitable products. See chapter 8 for more on pricing.

Please keep in mind that every business faces different costs. Do not assume that your costs are the same as those presented in our example. Every greenhouse firm faces its own unique set of circumstances and thus its own unique set of costs. Costs vary from greenhouse to greenhouse because of differences in climatic location, size, managerial skill and style, market channel, time of year, space utilization, wage rates, age and condition of facilities, and many other factors. Comparing your costs to industry averages will reveal areas where your costs are too high or areas where your costs are low and you have a market advantage. However, looking at industry averages is no substitute for doing your own cost accounting. With the availability of relatively low-cost computer software for small businesses, it is recommended that growers fully explore this avenue of record keeping.

8 Enhancing Greenhouse Profitability through Improved Pricing

Charles Hall—University of Tennessee

Pricing decisions are among the most difficult marketing-related decisions for the greenhouse firm, because prices must be high enough to cover costs and make a profit for your company but low enough to stimulate demand and sales. In addition, the price of a product affects the positioning of your firms' products within the marketplace. For example, a high-priced product (relative to the competition) has a connotation of high quality and is consistent with products that have special benefits. As you will see in this chapter, pricing plans require flexibility, discipline, and judgment to provide for a pricing structure that is competitive, complements the product's positioning, and maximizes profits.

Pricing Methods

Ideally, your pricing method should be based upon your operating budgets and your financial plans for the future. Setting the proper prices for your goods and services, with respect to what the market will accept, is the key to making your projected budgets and financial plans ultimately successful. However, there are almost as many pricing methods as there are companies in the greenhouse industry, and to say that one greenhouse's method or approach is superior to another's is not appropriate. What is appropriate is that you understand the theory and methodology of pricing for your own company as it applies to and reflects the industry.

Instead of developing or continuing to refine a price strategy based on the budgeted or planned cost of doing business, many companies devise methods that reflect what they perceive to be appropriate prices. Some of these methods are outlined below.

Many companies rely on the **judgment** of their owners and managers to determine what price to charge, rather than relying on the cost structure of the company. They believe that the opinion (and experience) of the managers and owners enables them to establish a price that is appropriate, even though the opinion may be out of touch with the reality of budgeted costs.

A price strategy known as **formula pricing** usually occurs when the management has heard of some other company using a formula for pricing. Such strategies are usually called "30 and 10" or "three times variable costs." With the "30 and 10" method, the company marks up its costs 30%, usually for overhead, and then adds another 10% for profit. With the "three times variable costs" method, the company simply determines its total variable costs and multiplies that figure by three to arrive at the selling price. In reality, this strategy may be appropriate for the "other" company, but it has no bearing on any other company unless the cost structures of both are identical.

Another method is setting the price based on **what the market will bear.** This strategy uses the insight and knowledge of a company's management to price the goods and services for "what they will go for." Here again is a method that lacks regard for the cost structure of the company, but it is perhaps the most aggressive method discussed here. This method takes full advantage of any opportunity to raise a price as high as possible. In contrast, a company using the judgment method may avoid inflating a price to higher than normal because of an opinion that the company should be conservative.

As mentioned previously, the ideal pricing method should be **based on costs** as outlined in operating budgets and financial plans for the future. With this method, company management devises a price strategy based on budgets and cost structures that will recover all costs, including overhead and profit. This ensures that the company can attain its financial goals.

The Best Pricing Strategy

The "based on costs" method is the only method addressed here that relies on the economic performance of the greenhouse operation as a basis of price strategy. The other methods rely on subjectivity and opinion rather than fact. Perhaps the best of all possible scenarios occurs when the pricing strategy is both market- and cost-oriented. This means you should consider what the market will bear as well as the production cost of each item. Your final price should reflect actual production costs, experience-based intuition, and knowledge of your competitors' prices. Thus, it is imperative to keep good records of direct production costs. These include:

- Supplies such as plugs, fertilizer, growing media, containers, and pesticides
- Labor (including Social Security benefits and workers' compensation)
- Cost of operating machinery and equipment (including repairs, lube, etc.)
- Anything else that directly contributes to the production cost of each plant

Total up your indirect production costs, such as insurance, interest, taxes, office supplies and equipment, and an allowance for unsold plants. Add in marketing costs, such as association dues; catalog production and mailing; related services (tagging, shipping, and so on); and marketing labor. Finally, add in profit and calculate the selling price for each plant.

Calculate the price of each crop individually (see chapter 7 for more information). Assign a given overhead cost to each plant category and divide by the number of plants you plan to sell. Because crops vary in growth rate, maintenance requirements, and loss factors, their production costs also vary. For instance, the cost of growing a 4-inch geranium is different than that of growing a 4-inch cyclamen. The pricing structure should reflect these differences.

When you know the true production costs of individual species, you can eliminate unprofitable plants or raise the price enough to cover your expenses and desired profit. You will also have a feel for how much a particular plant may be discounted before it becomes unprofitable. If there is excess production, management has the option of setting the price so that variable costs are covered and there is adequate margin for some contribution to fixed costs or overhead. In these short-run situations, if there is excess capacity, it is far better to take an order with less margin, because total company profit will be greater or profit loss will be less than if the order was not taken and the sale not made. In the long run, however, prices have to be established so that all costs (fixed and variable) are covered and there is a profit.

One thing to remember is that no matter how high your production costs are for a particular plant, its price cannot exceed its market value unless the services you provide substantially differentiate your operation from your competitors. Therein lies the true opportunity for greenhouse managers today in pricing their products: Develop intensive partnerships with retailers and landscaping firms, establish a competitive price at which an acceptable profit can be made, and differentiate your firm through quality and value-added services.

Pricing Challenges in the Greenhouse Industry

The challenge in directly applying economic theory to the greenhouse industry lies in the following considerations: First, there is absolutely no greenhouse that has perfect knowledge of its competitors' abilities to produce a product or the price at which a competitor will sell the product in the market. The industry is highly segmented, even within the same region and market, thus forcing companies to focus on portions of the market rather than the market as a whole. This segmentation has made it virtually impossible for the U.S. Department of Agriculture or any private agency to maintain extensive databases on historical prices. For economists and managers, this lack of industry pricing data is quite a handicap in making any sort of industry-wide price analysis.

Second, the time that is required in bringing greenhouse crops to market is perhaps the shortest within the green industry. Even if industry-wide pricing information were being collected, maintained, and disseminated at the time a crop is planted, the market information would be outdated and virtually useless by the time the product is available for sale. This phenomenon is accentuated by the fact that greenhouse managers must determine their product mix well before what little market information there is becomes available.

Lack of standardization further compounds the industry's pricing problem. A potted flowering plant from one greenhouse is often quite different from a potted flowering plant from another greenhouse. Unfortunately, unlike other agricultural industries, the greenhouse industry has few intermediaries to price and market its products, particularly when it comes to plants that are ultimately sold in garden centers. The number of brokers and middlemen in the distribution system is incredibly small compared to the number of suppliers and customers. And because of the variability of the product and the subjectivity of those who grade and set quality standards, there are no financial intermediaries. There is no such thing as "mum futures" that are traded or listed on a commodity exchange as with other agricultural crops.

Combine all of these factors, and one soon realizes that owners and managers of nurseries within this highly diversified industry have a difficult task indeed in setting prices that are realistic and appropriate to the cost structures of their operations. That is why adopting a management system that uses the internal information of the past, tempers that information with a realistic budget of the future, and defines a price strategy that coincides with that budget is the only way to ensure success. Adhering to the following list of considerations and cautions will be a step in that direction.

Things to Consider

- Review your pricing problems and opportunities and your marketing strategies before developing your pricing plan.
- Closely monitor the competition, and keep consistent records of your competitors' pricing.
- Be flexible. Be prepared to adjust to competitive pressures and the marketing environment.
- Be willing to change your price and use it as a tool for achieving marketing strategies.
- Use the pricing tool to communicate the positioning of your product.
- Test your price often. Test higher and lower prices, and monitor the response in test markets. Apply what you learn to your total system. However, make sure you test your pricing strategies for a long enough period to obtain realistic results.
- Remember, the more intangible the services you offer or unique your product, the more flexibility you will have in setting higher prices.
- Price your product to provide ultimate value to customers. Remember, you can still give real value through high price (for example, if the product is a little higher priced than the competitor's, but the customer receives a unique or better service).
- When determining your selling price, be aware of not only the obvious costs but also the hidden costs (such as empty bench space, death losses, shrinkage through employee or customer theft, etc.).

Things to Be Cautious Of

- Don't look at pricing as static. The cost of doing business and the competitive activity in the marketplace are not fixed. Your pricing shouldn't be either.
- Don't set pricing without first determining how it will affect sales, margins, and the ability of the company to cover variable and fixed costs.
- Don't be afraid to use price to achieve other marketing goals. Successful companies often plan for a period of lower prices in an effort to increase trial and build the customer base. Though profitability is reduced temporarily, it is often offset by a sustained period of repeated purchases at full price by the expanded customer base.

- While being flexible, make sure you don't confuse potential purchasers with constantly changing prices.
- Don't overreact to the competition. Before you change your long-run pricing strategy, wait to see if the competitive price changes are temporary or permanent. At the same time, learn to anticipate and react to short-run competitive price changes.
- If you are attempting to build an image based on quality or value, don't lower an already competitive price; instead, put greater emphasis on the quality of your product.

9 Enhancing Greenhouse Profitability through Improved Financial Analysis

P.J. van Blokland—University of Florida

This chapter describes financial tools greenhouse owners can use to make sensible financial decisions about their firms. Descriptions of the tools are not exhaustive, and further study and practice beyond what is presented here will be necessary.

Times have changed. It used to be that good production practices led to good farm income. Today, however, greenhouse firms need to make good marketing and financing decisions as well. It is not enough to do the job right. It is much more important to do the right job, and this requires modern management methods. This chapter assumes that the manager and owner of the firm are the same person.

Management in any job consists of using information to make decisions to help the firm meet its objectives. Consequently, the manager needs to know what the objectives are. Objectives need to be written down and quantified in terms of numbers and time. "Make a profit" is not an objective, but "Make $100,000 net income by the end of December three years hence" is. And in setting objectives, the manager must realize where the firm stands today and how it got there. Therefore, an important part of good management is linking the past with the future by making sound decisions today. This chapter describes some of the main financial tools to help managers make such links.

Figure 9.1 presents the essential financial tools for any firm. These tools provide the information necessary to make the most of production, marketing, and financing decisions in the firm. The diagram starts with the information the manager thinks he or she needs. This information is digested and used to state the firm's objectives. The diagram then separates into two parts. The left-hand side, or the recording section, shows what has happened to the firm over time. These events were recorded and analyzed to write the objectives of the firm. The right-hand side, or the management section, shows what might happen to the firm if it meets its current and future objectives. The left- and right-hand sides are linked by monitoring—in other words, by comparing what actually happened with what the manager thought would happen. The manager must make decisions on any differences between the two. Of course, there will always be a difference, for no one is clairvoyant. The real job is to make the right decision on the difference.

For instance, suppose that the manager thought, based on historical performance, that the second-quarter greenhouse cash sales margin over cash costs would be $400,000, and the margin actually was $300,000. This falls $100,000 short, and that $100,000 was probably committed to future uses. The manager may have lined up resources for certain purpose and now has bills to pay instead. The task now becomes finding out why there was a cash margin difference of 25% and deciding what should be done about it (doing nothing is still a decision). This is not easy, but it is real management. The tools described below will help in this decision-making process and, if necessary, help in modifying future objectives.

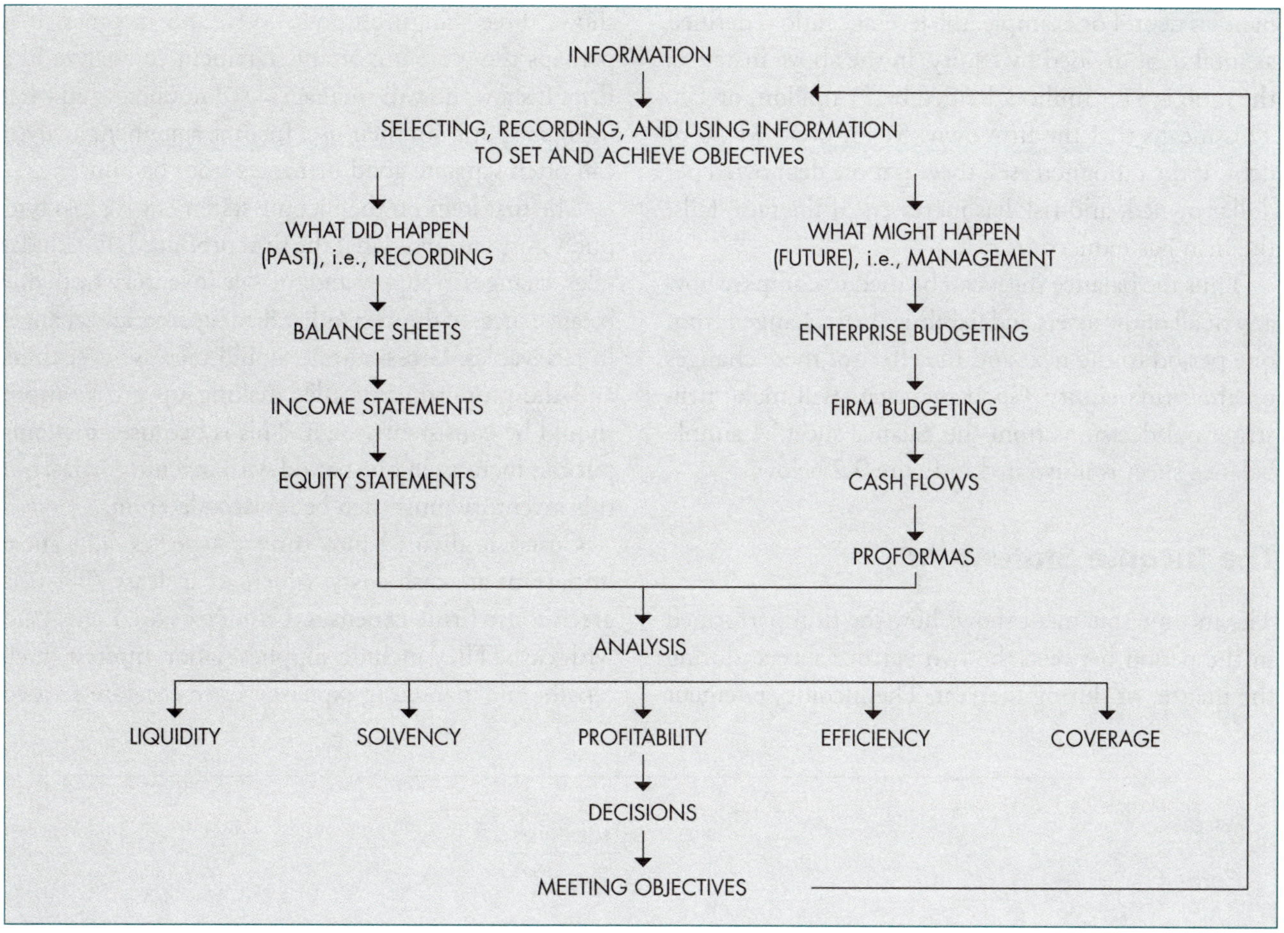

Figure 9.1. *The essential financial tools of a firm*

The Balance Sheet

The balance sheet presents a picture of the firm at one point in time. This is an important point to digest. Because the balance sheet is a snapshot of the firm on one day, the firm's owners, correctly and legally, make this statement look as good as they can in order to impress their readers. People dress well when they are interviewed or inspected. Firm owners want to look good when they produce their balance sheets.

The balance sheet shows three things: assets, liabilities, and equity. Assets are what the firm owns and are usually divided into three categories in agriculture: current, intermediate, and long-term. Current assets can be or soon will be turned into cash. They include items like inventory for sale, supply inventory, cash, cash equivalents (such as savings accounts, stocks, bonds, mutual funds), and receivables. Intermediate assets usually consist of vehicles, equipment, machinery, and nonpermanent buildings and structures. Long-term assets are permanent buildings and land.

Liabilities are what the firm owes. These also fall into three categories: current, intermediate, and long-term. Current liabilities are what the firm owes in the period between now and the next balance sheet. These would be the quarterly bills for a firm that reports quarterly, or annual expenses for firms with a yearly set of accounts. Current liabilities include the principal and interest on operating loans, payables, and the current principal and interest portion of intermediate and long-term debt—what the firm owes in the next period on its notes and mortgages. Intermediate liabilities are what the firm owes on notes after deducting the current portion. Likewise, long-term liabilities are the remaining mortgages owed after meeting the current portion.

Equity is what the firm owns. It is calculated by subtracting all the liabilities from the firm's assets. For example, if the assets are \$2.5 million and liabilities are \$1.5 million, the firm's equity is \$1 million. Equity is a key number for managerial scrutiny. Managers want to see steady equity growth, period after period. Equity is also used in various ratios to see how the firm handles debt. For example, the leverage ratio is defined as total debt divided by equity. In the above instance, the ratio is $1.5 million divided by $1 million, or 1.5. This means that the firm owns $1 for every $1.50 of debt. If the ratio increases, there is more debt owed per dollar owned, and risk has increased. If the ratio falls, the firm has reduced its risk.

Thus the balance sheet can be used to compare how any or all of the assets and liabilities have changed from one period to the next and the effect of these changes on the firm's equity. Good managers will make firm structural decisions from the balance sheet. A simple balance sheet is illustrated in figure 9.2 below.

The Income Statement

The income statement shows how the firm performed in the period between the two balance sheets, during the quarter or during the year. The income statement shows three things: outputs, costs, and incomes. It is perhaps the most important statement to analyze in a firm. It shows how the manager used resources and what he or she got from their use. Income statement analysis can often separate good managers from bad ones.

The first item on the income statement is gross output. Gross output is what the firm produced. It includes sales, changes in supply and for-sale inventory from one balance sheet to the next, other firm income, and changes in receivables. Gross output should increase over time, and the proportion of sales making up gross output should be consistently high. This is because gross output can increase in one period with inventory sales, but this inventory must then be replaced later on.

Costs are divided into three categories. The most important are **cash costs**, which are at least 70% of a greenhouse firm's expenses. Cash costs are items paid with cash. They include supplies, labor, interest, fuel, repairs, and marketing expenses. Cash costs are divided

Assets		Liabilities	
Current		*Current*	
cash + cash equivalents	______	payables	______
sale inventory	______	operating loans	______
supply inventory	______	current portion of notes	______
other inventory	______	current portion of mortgages	______
receivables	______	other loans	______
Intermediate		*Intermediate*	
vehicles	______	vehicle notes	______
equipment	______	equipment notes	______
temporary buildings	______	building notes	______
Long-term		*Long-term*	
permanent buildings	______	building mortgages	______
land	______	land mortgages	______
TOTAL ASSETS	______	TOTAL LIABILITIES	______

TOTAL ASSETS – TOTAL LIABILITIES = EQUITY (NET WORTH)

Figure 9.2. *A simple balance sheet*

into four or five major categories for analysis (chemicals and fertilizers; labor, Social Security, and associated taxes and expenses; marketing expenses; interest). These categories are not standard but are determined by each firm. The idea is to account for about 80% of cash costs in the categories, and to follow what happens to each category.

Gross output minus cash costs equals gross margin. Gross margin shows whether the firm can cover its cash costs and, if it can, how much is left to cover the rest of its commitments. Gross margin is an exceedingly useful concept that can be used for individual enterprises and for the whole firm. Again, it is important to follow the gross margin of the different enterprises and use this information to make changes in enterprise operation.

The second major cost is **depreciation**. This cost is the annual rate allowed by the Internal Revenue Service (IRS) to write off depreciable capital assets. Depreciation is a real cost, although the firm does not pay it until it replaces its capital assets. Capital assets that can be depreciated include buildings, machinery, and vehicles. Until these assets are replaced, the depreciation allowances by the IRS add cash to the firm. This "additional" cash is most easily seen in the cash flow.

The third cost category is **overhead**. This category is usually disregarded by firms or used as a catch-all for miscellaneous items. All overhead items can be put in cash or depreciation costs. But because overhead is relatively unproductive compared with the other two costs, overhead should be recorded separately. Overhead items include office expenses, business education and publications, lawyer and accountant fees, business travel, and client entertainment.

There is a tendency for firms that have had good years to expand their travel and entertainment overhead when that money might be better spent on cash cost items; therefore, it is advisable to track the cost shares of the three types of costs over time to see where firm expenditures go. Rules of thumb are usually incorrect, but a "typical" greenhouse firm might have 75% of its costs as cash, 18% as depreciation, and the remaining 7% as overhead. Any marked deviation from the firm's historical trends needs to be investigated and explained.

Cash costs plus depreciation plus overhead equals total costs. Gross output minus total costs equals net firm income. A positive net firm income shows the firm has covered all of its costs, but net firm income is not profit. The firm still has other commitments. Net firm income is essentially equivalent to taxable income for a noncorporation, because property taxes, road taxes, and other firm taxes are cash costs. A high net firm income means higher taxes, which might encourage the manager to purchase some needed depreciable capital asset. Depreciation reduces the net firm income and the tax bill.

Net firm income minus the owners' taxes and Social Security taxes provides net income. This is the bottom line of any firm. To see how a firm is doing, follow its net income over time. A firm's net income can only be used for three things: the owners' salaries, reinvesting in the firm, and principal payments. The owners' salaries include what the owners withdraw from the firm for living expenses, including vacations, purchases for private items, education, etc. Owners' salaries are the equivalent of dividends. Any capital purchases must come from net income. Principal payments are settled with the firm's net income. Interest on principal is a cash cost. The corporate equivalent of principal plus investments is called retained earnings. Figure 9.3 (page 42) illustrates an income statement.

The income statement shows the money coming into the firm and where the money goes in the firm in the period between the two balance sheets. Understand that any firm can adapt the cost framework in the statement to suit its specific needs. The items listed under each cost are examples only. Realize also that the net income shows how the money after total costs and owners' taxes was spent. It is not a residual, and there is nothing left after its three uses. Put another way, net income minus investing in the firm and principal payments equals what the owners withdrew as salary.

Good analysis of this statement will include trends in gross output, costs, and incomes and the changes in the components of each that caused these trends. Decisions will be made based on these changes, and objectives will be rewritten as cause and effect are determined.

The Statement of Owner Equity

The statement of owner equity links the beginning and ending balance sheets with the income statement to show how owner equity has changed over time. Owner equity is a key number to monitor. It shows how much

Gross Output

sales ______
other income to firm ______
change in supply inventory ______
change in sales inventory ______
change in receivables ______
Total ______

Cash Costs

category 1 (for example, chemicals and fertilizers) ______
category 2 (for example, all hired labor expenses) ______
category 3 (for example, transportation, fuel, repairs) ______
category 4 (for example, all marketing expenses) ______
category 5 (for example, all other cash costs) ______
Total ______

GROSS OUTPUT – CASH COSTS = GROSS MARGIN ______

Depreciation

vehicles ______
machinery and equipment ______
buildings ______
all other depreciable assets ______
Total ______

Overhead

office expenses ______
salaries and fees ______
business travel/entertainment ______
all other overhead ______
Total ______

Total Costs

cash costs + depreciation + overhead (see totals from above)
Total ______

TOTAL GROSS OUTPUT – TOTAL COSTS = NET FIRM INCOME ______

Owners' Taxes

income taxes ______
Social Security taxes ______
other taxes ______
Total ______

NET FIRM INCOME – OWNERS' TAXES = NET INCOME ______

Net Income

principal payments ______
reinvesting ______
owners' salaries ______

Figure 9.3. *A sample income statement format*

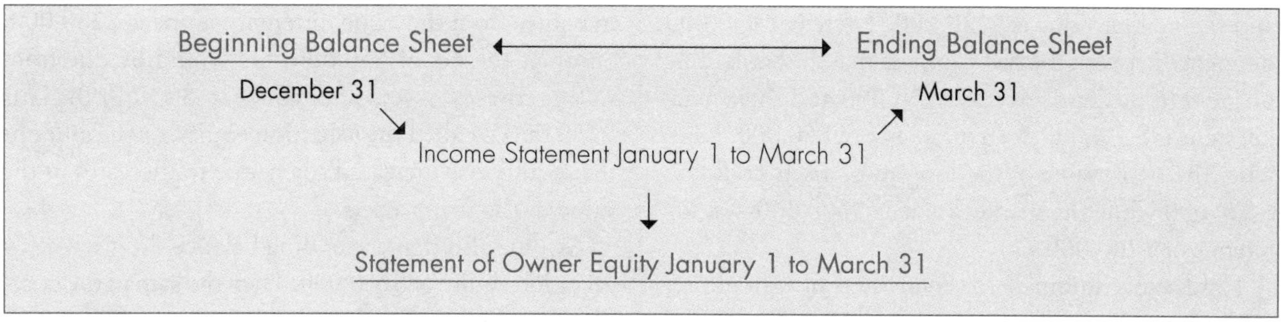

Figure 9.4. *Linkages within a statement of owner equity*

of the firm is owned by the owners, who hope to see continuing equity growth over time. Equity growth probably ranks second to net income as the most important indicator of firm success.

This statement has three useful pieces of information. It shows (1) how equity is increased by paying off principal and investing in the firm (adding retained earnings, in accounting language); (2) how equity is depleted by taking salary from the firm; and (3) how inflation and deflation affect equity as asset values change.

Figure 9.4 shows the linkages for a quarterly set of statements. The statement starts with the equity recorded in the beginning balance sheet on December 31. Say this is $500,000. The net income from the income statement for the next quarter is added to this equity. With a net income of $50,000, equity increases to $550,000. Subtract owners' salaries of $20,000, and the revised equity is now $530,000. So, in answer to point number one in the paragraph above, the statement shows that equity increased in the firm by $30,000, which came from paying off principal and reinvesting. (Note that the $50,000 net income went on $20,000 salary and $30,000 principal and investing.)

The second point is showing how equity is depleted by drawing salary. The withdrawal of $20,000 for salaries reduced equity by that amount. Obviously, the more the owners withdraw, the lower the equity growth will be. This may seem trite, but it is an important point. Owners have to have enough to live on and to enjoy themselves. Only they can decide whether the increased enjoyment is worth the reduction of equity growth. The statement of owner equity shows the relative effects clearly. Some 40% of the quarter's net income went on salary, so the remaining 60% was available to increase equity.

The third point is showing changes in asset valuation due to external factors, which are usually combined under the rubric of inflation. It is possible for a firm's equity growth to be entirely due to inflation. If, for example, land prices were to double, then the firm's real estate would be worth twice as much as it was before, and equity growth would be correspondingly impressive. On the other hand, if inflation were to decrease, equity growth would fall correspondingly, and the firm would not look so good. This artificial type of equity growth must be realized to avoid bad decisions. In order to work out asset valuation changes correctly, the manager needs a balance sheet to record assets on both book and market-value bases.

Book value can be measured in three ways, depending on the type of asset. One measure is what the owner has invested in the items. This measure will apply to most of the firm's inventory items—for example, valuing a 10-inch pot plant at $4.50, because that is the sum of the cash, depreciation, and overhead costs and the management that went into it. A second way to measure book value is to use what the item cost the firm. This measurement is often used for nondepreciable assets—for example, $3,500 for an additional acre of land or $10 for a plant that the greenhouse will subsequently add value to. The third way to measure book value is to use the current depreciated value of the asset—for example, a three-year-old tractor that has a depreciated value of $50,000 is simply valued at that amount.

The market value of an asset is what the firm could get for that asset if it were sold soon. Market value is mostly greater than book value. Current assets are usually valued at either what has been invested in them (book) or what they could be sold for in the marketplace. Suppose the book value of these assets is $90,000 and the market value is $120,000. There is a $30,000 difference between the two. Suppose that the book value of the intermediate assets is $150,000 and their market value is $200,000, for a difference of $50,000. Likewise, the book value of the long-term assets could be $400,000 while the market value is $600,000—a difference of $200,000.

Land assets dominate the total assets of agriculture, even in greenhouse firms. Land cannot be depreciated, so the "book" value of the land is either the original purchase price or, if it was purchased generations ago, the latest assessment of the value of the land. The market value is what the land can fetch in today's market. Usually land values signal inflation in agricultural markets.

So the book value of all the firm's assets in the example above is $90,000 plus $150,000 plus $400,000, which equals $640,000. The market value of its assets is $120,000 plus $200,000 plus $600,000, which equals $920,000. The difference between the two is $280,000. Taxes will be due on the differences in the noncurrent assets if they are sold. With a tax bracket of 20%, the tax due equals $50,000 [($600,000 + $200,000) – ($150,000 + $400,000) × 0.20].

Assume that all these asset values are shown in the beginning balance sheet. If liabilities are $140,000, then the cost or book equity is $640,000 – $140,000 = $500,000. The book equity is the equity earned by the firm up to that point in time. The market value equity is $920,000 – $140,000 = $780,000. This equity is what the owners would get if they sold all their assets and met all their pretax liabilities. Therefore the gain in equity from the value difference alone is $280,000. Subtract the tax of $50,000 that would be due from selling these assets, and you get $230,000. This $230,000 is called the valuation equity, or the amount that equity has increased solely due to increases in the value of the firm's assets.

Assume also that the ending balance sheet records a valuation equity of $260,000. Then the gain in the quarter from changes in asset valuation is only $260,000 – $230,000 = $30,000. The three functions of the statement of owner equity are summarized in figure 9.5.

The firm's equity increased $30,000 during the quarter from the firm's production. But it also increased $60,000 from changes in the valuation of the firm's assets. The former shows the results of the manager's work and the latter shows the external factors, which are largely driven by inflation. Owners can use either or both numbers as they like. The important thing is to know the difference between the two and what causes these differences.

Analytical Tools

After the historic performance of a firm is presented in balance sheets, income statements, and the statement of owner equity, the statements must be analyzed. There are five basic sets of tools used in analysis: liquidity, solvency, profitability, efficiency, and repayment capacity.

Liquidity

Liquidity indicates how "liquid" a business is. In other words, how difficult is it to raise cash? The definition

		Book basis	Market basis
Owner equity in beginning balance sheet		500,000	780,000
1. Net income during the quarter	plus	50,000	50,000
2. Salary taken during quarter	minus	(20,000)	(20,000)
3. Change in valuation equity			
– ending balance sheet...+ $260,000			
– beginning balance sheet...– $230,000			
– total change	plus		30,000
Owner equity in ending balance sheet		530,000	840,000
Change in owner equity		30,000	60,000

Figure 9.5. *Summary of statement of owner equity*

of liquidity is the ability to meet liabilities when they become due. The due liabilities are the current liabilities listed on the balance sheet. The cash to pay them comes from the current assets listed on the same balance sheet. There must be enough current assets, as cash, to pay current liabilities. If there are enough, then the firm is liquid. If there are not enough, then the firm is illiquid. Today, all firms must stay liquid, so cash is the most important asset there is. Good managers spend a lot of time making certain that their firms are safely liquid.

Working Capital. Working capital (inventory plus accounts receivable plus cash) is one of the major tools in the liquidity toolbox. It is calculated by subtracting current liabilities from current assets. For example, if the firm's current assets are $80,000 and current liabilities are $50,000, then there is $30,000 in working capital. In other words, after paying all the due debts, there will be $30,000 left. The firm is liquid, and that is good news.

Quick Working Capital. Some current assets may not be quite as liquid as others. For instance, growing crops are not as easy to sell (that is, not as liquid) as crops waiting to go to market. Nothing is as liquid as cash.

Quick working capital is a tool that takes the "stickiness" of some of the current assets into account to give a more realistic picture of how much cash is actually available. Only current assets that can be sold quickly without a discount are included. These include cash; savings; investments in stocks, bonds, and mutual funds; receivables that can be realistically realized quickly; and any inventory that is at or close to the point of sale. There will be times when the working capital of a firm looks substantial, but the quick working capital is negative. In other words, the firm is not as liquid as it originally seemed.

Current Ratio. The current ratio is calculated by dividing current assets by current liabilities. Thus if the current ratio of a firm at a specific point in time is 1.25 to 1, this means that there is $1.25 to cover every $1 of debt due. Most firms will find it safe to keep their current ratio between 2 and 3, meaning that they have $2 to $3 available to cover every $1 in current liabilities. If the ratio falls below 2, the manager should make sure that the firm can get liquid when it needs to. And if the ratio rises above 3, then the firm has cash available for investing.

Current Debt Ratio. The current debt ratio (CDR), the final tool in the liquidity toolbox, is found by dividing current liabilities by total liabilities. It shows what proportion of the entire firm's debt, both principal and interest, is due in the next period. For example, if current liabilities are $35,000 and total debt is $150,000, the CDR equals 35,000 ÷ 150,000 = 0.23. This means that 23 cents of every dollar owed is due in the following period. Obviously it is hard to generalize about any "correct" ratio, because it depends completely on the firm's debt load. But for a typical firm with a normal debt load, it is probably useful to keep the annual ratio below 0.1. A CDR of 0.1 means that the firm must pay about 10% of its debt annually, so that its current debt level would be cleared in ten years. Most firms will find this a difficult objective to achieve.

Solvency

Solvency is a long-run concept. It shows whether the firm can meet all of its debts if it sells all of its assets. If the assets are greater than the liabilities, then the firm is solvent. If assets are less than liabilities, then the firm is insolvent or bankrupt.

Equity. This is the single best measurement of solvency. If the firm has equity, it is solvent. Perhaps the most useful indicator of a firm's progress is a good equity trend.

Leverage Ratio. The leverage ratio is calculated by dividing total debt by equity. For example, if the firm's total debts are $200,000 and equity is $100,000, then the leverage ratio is 200,000 ÷ 100,000, or 2. In other words, the firm has $2 in debt for every $1 that it owns. Most firms will find it preferable to keep this ratio to a maximum of 1. However, it depends on the situation the firm is in and the objectives and ages of the owners. Usually young owners will have higher leverage ratios than more mature owners. A high leverage ratio is nothing to be ashamed of, but it is something to get out of.

Profitability

Profitability is a word that everyone recognizes but few can define. The most obvious commonsense measures of profitability are the incomes that were outlined in the section on the income statement—namely, net firm income and net income (see page 40). Recall that net income is the bottom line for the firm.

Return on Equity. Return on equity, perhaps the most important trend to look for after net income, shows the return on owned money in the business. It is calculated using the formula:

(net income – owners' salaries ÷ beginning equity) x 100 = ROE

For example, suppose the firm's net income for the quarter was $40,000. The owners withdrew $16,000 for salary, and the equity at the start of the quarter was $300,000. The firm's ROE is therefore

[(40,000 – 16,000) ÷ 300,000] x 100 = 8%

Return on Assets. Return on assets is calculated using the formula:

(net firm income + interest paid – owners' salary) x 100 ÷ beginning assets = ROA

The interest paid on debts is added back, because the firm borrowed money to buy assets and is paying interest as a cost of borrowing. The interest represents the return from that asset using the borrowed money. Thus part of the asset is financed with debt and part with equity, and the manager wants to know what the total return on that asset is. Therefore, the interest must be added back to calculate the total return. Hopefully the return will be greater than the cost of borrowing. It is not sensible to borrow at 10% if the investment is returning 6%. This will happen if ROE is less than ROA—the firm is earning less than it is paying to borrow funds.

For example, suppose the firm had a net firm income of $50,000 during the quarter, paid interest of $10,000, and withdrew salary of $16,000. The assets at the beginning of the quarter were $600,000. The ROA is therefore

(50,000 +10,000 – 16,000) x 100 ÷ 600,000 = 7.33%

Efficiency

Efficiency is perhaps the most familiar tool to greenhouse managers. Most efficiency tools refer to the relationship between inputs and outputs. Examples include yields per acre, hours of labor per square foot, cash cost expenses per square foot, sales per week, boxes picked per hour of labor, and so forth. Such measures are often kept by firms. They will not be presented in detail here, except to emphasize their importance.

Operations Ratios. Operations ratios are particularly useful in examining how costs change over time. This tool uses percentage ratios that always add up to 100%. The components are: (1) cash costs, excluding interest; (2) depreciation; (3) interest; (4) owners' taxes and Social Security; (5) other costs not already counted; and (6) net income. All of these components come from the income statement. Adding the six components to-

Components	$	%
Cash costs, excluding interest	70,000	58
Depreciation	10,000	9
Interest	12,000	10
Taxes and Social Security	4,000	3
Overhead	4,000	3
Net income*	20,000	17
Gross Output	120,000	100

* This is the residual from subtracting all the costs from the gross output.

Figure 9.6. *A quarterly income statement*

gether gives the firm's gross output. For an example, see the quarterly income statement in figure 9.6.

The interpretation of figure 9.6 is that 17% of the firm's gross output results in net income; 58% goes on cash costs, excluding interest; 10% goes on interest; and so on. Put another way, for every dollar that the firm generated in the quarter, 17 cents was net income; 58 cents went on cash costs, excluding interest; etc. The most useful thing about this tool is spotting trends. If, for example, interest costs took an increasing share of each gross output dollar, the manager has some decisions to make.

Asset Turnover. Firms, and greenhouse firms in particular, have to know how quickly they turn their assets over. The classic definition for asset turnover is gross output divided by average total assets. It shows how assets are used to generate output. The greater the ratio, the better the assets are used. For example, if the firm produces $1 million gross output in a year and its average asset valuation is $5 million, the turnover ratio is 20%. One fifth of its assets turn over annually. But because of the almost unique asset fixity in agriculture (that is, the land domination of assets)—even in the greenhouse business—perhaps another denominator is more useful. For those firms that have more than 30% of their total asset values in land, remove land from the denominator and work with the remaining assets. Then compare the turnovers with and without land.

Labor Productivity. Labor productivity is a particularly important ratio for greenhouse firms. It can be calculated by dividing the firm's gross output by the labor cost of the firm. For some firms, it might be interesting to include the owners' salaries in the denominator as well.

Repayment Capacity

There are three main repayment capacity measurements, and they all focus on how the firm can pay its debts. Note that these three measures all assume that operating debt will be repaid as the output is sold. So unless any operating debt is carried over from the previous period, all operating debt, both principal and interest, is excluded from the formulae.

Coverage Ratio. This ratio is found by the following formula:

$$\frac{\text{net income + depreciation + interest} - \text{owners' salaries and taxes}}{\text{annual principal and interest payments}} = \text{coverage ratio}$$

The higher the ratio, the easier it is for the firm to meet its debt commitments. If the ratio is 1, the firm can just meet its debts. It also means, to some extent, that the firm is living off of depreciation to service the debt. In other words, the firm cannot replace any of the capital depreciation with new purchases. Anything greater than 1 gives the firm room to do other things.

Capital and Debt Ratio. This ratio is essentially the next step up from the coverage ratio. It shows whether the firm can both meet its debt and afford to replace the capital assets lost in producing its net income. The formula is:

$$\text{net income + depreciation} - \text{owners' salaries and taxes} - \text{principal payments} = \text{capital and debt ratio}$$

Debt-to-Income Ratio. This is calculated as follows:

$$\frac{\text{average total liabilities}}{\text{net firm income}} = \text{debt-to-income ratio}$$

The average total liabilities is calculated by adding the liabilities of the beginning and ending balance sheets together and dividing by two. The ratio shows the number of times that the firm's debt exceeds its net firm income. For example, if liabilities are $300,000 and the net firm income is $50,000, the ratio is 6. This means that, at the current rate, it would take six years for the income to equal debt. If the ratio falls to 5, then income leverage is reduced, and the firm has reduced its risk. If the ratio rises, then income leverage is increasing. This increases the firm's risk, because it becomes increasingly difficult to service the debt from current income.

Summary of What Did Happen

Managers, by necessity, look at past performance to evaluate how the firm is doing. This synopsis, using balance sheets, income statements, and statements of owner equity, provides the raw data for the five analytical tools of liquidity, solvency, profitability, efficiency, and repayment capacity. The manager is expected to produce answers from this analysis that will show whether the firm is meeting its objectives and help in formulating new objectives. But, unfortunately, analysis is neither entirely scientific nor precise. A manager must use art or intelligent guesswork in analyzing the financial health of a firm, much like a doctor assesses and makes conclusions on the physical health of a patient.

Perhaps the most important part of this assessment is estimating what the firm (or the patient) will look like in the future. It is this estimate that produces the objectives of the firm by bringing past performance and future predictions together. Analysis of past performance and knowledge of the present situation formulates what the firm can do in the future. This requires the use of the tools on the right-hand side of figure 9.1 (page 39), and those tools are described below.

Budgeting

Budgeting is trying to plan future expenditures and match them in some way with future sales and other dollar inflows. It is probably the single most important function in running a firm. No one knows the future, so budgeting results are usually wrong. But it is essential to try.

A budget is a map for the future of the firm. No one should go on a journey into the unknown without a map. And as with taking a journey, budgeting involves estimating change as circumstances change.

The procedure starts with budgeting the firm's individual enterprises. These enterprises are then added together to make the firm's budget. The firm's budget is then used to produce the cash flow for the firm.

Enterprise Budget

A generalized enterprise budget is shown in figure 9.7. The blanks under each category are where the individual items making up that category are entered. For example, the items of fertilizer, chemicals, labor, etc., would go under cash costs. The sums of the different categories are shown by a capital letter.

Note that sales have proxied for gross output. If it is possible to budget the gross output of the enterprise, then do it. But budgeting is difficult enough anyway, and as sales are usually easier to estimate, they are a good proxy for gross output. The enterprise budget figure shows that each enterprise has to play its part in meeting all the firm's outlays. These outlays include not only the cash, depreciation, and overhead costs but also owners' taxes, salaries, principal payments, and funds for reinvesting in the firm. Therefore, if "L" is positive, the firm has a good enterprise to consider. If it is negative, the firm should produce something else. Obviously, there is a limited choice for any firm. But the main point is that no enterprise should be produced in the long run if it cannot pay all the freight that is presented in figure 9.7.

Assume that the enterprise can generate a positive "L." This is a necessary but not sufficient reason for the manager to produce it. There are at least four questions that must be answered before the enterprise is produced:

1. Are there enough resources available to produce it (sufficient land, labor, debt and equity capital, and managerial ability)?
2. Is there a market for this enterprise, and what must the firm do to get the enterprise to that market?
3. What must be done to the enterprise before it is marketable (how must it be prepared, graded, packaged, transported, etc.)?
4. What are the production, financing, and marketing risks involved (yield; cost and price volatility; capital availability; and the effects of weather, pests, diseases, breakdowns, strikes)?

If the answers to these questions look good, then repeat the process with other possible enterprises, select the ones that look the most profitable, and combine them into a firm budget.

Combining Selected Enterprises to Make a Firm Budget

The procedure for making a firm budget is to list the enterprises in a table, complete the row names in the table, calculate the net firm income from each enterprise, and add across the table to produce the firm budget.

A reasonable layout for this exercise is shown in figure 9.8 (page 50), which also includes the projected numbers for the five enterprises and a total. The layout lists each enterprise's contribution to the firm and how each contribution is shared among the outlays.

ANTICIPATED SALES AND COSTS OF PRODUCING ONE (UNIT) OF ENTERPRISE (NAME) IN (WHERE) IN (YEAR)

			$ per Unit
Sales			
Anticipated (yield____) x Anticipated (price___)		=	A ________
Costs and Indicators			
(1) Cash costs	________		
	________		
	Total cash costs	=	B ________
Gross Margin	(A) – (B)	=	C ________
(2) Depreciation	________		
	________		
	Total depreciation	=	D ________
(3) Overhead (prorated)		=	E ________
Total Costs	(B) + (D) + (E)	=	F ________
Net Firm Income (A) – (F)		=	G ________
(4) Owners' estimated taxes and Social Security		=	H ________
Net Income (G) – (H)		=	I ________
Minus			
1. Salary to owners		=	J ________
2. Principal payments		=	K ________
Equals			
Amount left for buying assets	(I) – (J + K)	=	L ________

Figure 9.7. *A general enterprise budget*

Note: The blanks under each category are where the individual items making up that category are entered. For example, the items of fertilizer, chemicals, labor, etc., would go under cash costs. The sums of the different categories are shown by a capital letter.

Based on these figures, the owner would expect the firm to have $800,000 in sales; $470,000 in cash costs; $115,000 in capital assets as depreciation; $45,000 in overhead; $34,000 in income and Social Security taxes; and $136,000 in net income to allocate for salaries, principal, and reinvestment in the firm. Because firms vary considerably in net income allocations, allocations are not shown here. Given a salary of $50,000, there is approximately $86,000 remaining for principal and investing. Note that reinvesting will reduce income taxes if depreciable assets are purchased.

The budget estimates come from experience, records, and current events. There are, however, some simple guidelines for these estimates. With many greenhouse firms, cash costs are typically 75–80% of total costs. Likewise, depreciation is about 15–20%, and overhead is what is left. Net income is often about 15% of gross sales. These are guidelines only, but they are useful for

Categories	Enterprise Budgets 1	2	3	4	5	Firm Budget Total
Sales	250	200	150	100	100	800
Cash Costs	150	120	80	60	60	470
Depreciation	36	29	22	14	14	115
Overhead	14	11	8	6	6	45
Total Costs	200	160	110	80	80	630
Net Firm Income	50	40	40	20	20	170
Tax + Social Security	10	8	8	4	4	34
Net Income	40	32	32	16	16	136

Figure 9.8. *Methodology for developing enterprise and firm budgets (in thousands $)*

budgeting purposes. If events change, then the budget must be adjusted to reflect the changes. Estimates are always hard to do, and they are usually wrong. But they are the best tool available for the future, and they become more accurate as the future gets closer to the present.

The most important asset today is cash. Managers need to know when they will need cash and when it comes into the firm. The next step, therefore, is to produce a cash flow.

The Firm Cash Flow

Cash flow is a planning tool that stems from the firm's budget and is the final planning tool before resources are allocated to produce the firm's enterprises. The cash flow plans the future inflows and outflows of cash in the firm over a specific time period. It also shows cash in the business at the beginning and ending of a period.

Examples of cash coming in include sales, new borrowing, other firm income, and new equity. Examples of cash leaving the business include cash costs, principal payments, owners' salaries, asset purchases, and owners' income taxes and Social Security.

The cash flow does three things. It predicts the future, which is what most managers use it for. More important, it monitors predictions by comparing the original estimates with what actually happened. Finally, it helps managers make decisions on the difference between predicted and actual results.

For example, suppose that at the beginning of the year August sales were predicted to be $60,000, but at the end of August the actual sales were $40,000, or 33% less than the estimate. What decision should the manager make? Adjust subsequent sales to reflect the difference? Do nothing? The answer, of course, depends on why sales were down. If it was because the market price fell or yields or quality was down, then some future adjustments will be necessary. But if the plants were not quite ready for sale, then perhaps only September's numbers should be adjusted.

If cash is unavailable when it is expected, then there is more to consider than sales. Cash outflows were originally matched to inflows. If inflows fall, cash commitments cannot be met. Commitments include debt service, payables, and salaries. Consequently, other cash sources must be tapped to meet commitments. A properly used cash flow shows what is happening and suggests what the consequences will be when predictions must be changed. Cash flow is constantly changing and provides the manager the cash map necessary for cash management.

Cash flow forms vary, and no single basic form fits every firm, unlike the balance sheet and the income statement. It is more important to have a good cash flow system than worry about form uniformity. The system should run for three years, with the nearby year having all details in possibly 100 row names and the last year having only a few major summaries in perhaps ten row names. The nearby year uses monthly columns, always keeping 12 months ahead; thus as one month expires, the same month in the following year comes in. The second cash flow is done quarterly so that there are five main columns (four quarters and a total) and maybe 20 row names. The final cash flow is an annual flow with just one column and perhaps ten rows. The row reduction is for two reasons. First, it is unreasonable to expect to predict the future in detail three years ahead. Consequently, summarizing the major sales and cost categories is the best that most people can do. Second, it is easy to fail to see the forest for the trees. Thus, focusing on the major items helps to provide the detail for the nearby cash flow. A simplified cash flow layout is shown in figure 9.9. This can be modified to fit the system in any firm.

Any one of the row names in figure 9.9 can be divided into its components to provide detail or be summarized to present a succinct picture. The cash costs, for example, could and possibly should have 30–40 rows in the first cash flow and maybe four or five in the annual flow. It may be useful to use a third or a separate loan section in the figure to itemize each loan and keep a running total of the current debt situation.

The cash flow shows the debt repayments. It shows when cash is available and when it is not. Use the cash flow to present sensible debt scheduling to lenders. It is not the lender but the firm's cash flow that shows what can be done in paying interest and principal. Make sure that all parties involved understand this. The cash flow also incorporates new events. As events change, so will the firm's results. Thus, the cash flow must be changed constantly to reflect changes and to reflect increasing knowledge of what will happen to cash inflows and cash outflows. The alterations show the results of the changes.

Cash flow shows when the firm can afford to buy assets. If the cash is not there but an asset is needed, it shows the consequences of increasing the debt load to obtain the asset. It also shows how much salary can be drawn by the owners and the consequences of paying salary rather than spending the cash on other things.

Monitoring compares predictions with what actually happened. Predictions may be wrong, and the farther away the predictions, the less accurate they may be. But the firm has to buy and use resources such as fertilizer and labor before it produces sales. These are

	Time period 1	Time period 2
Opening cash balance	______	______
Cash In		
Sales	______	______
Other cash income	______	______
New borrowing	______	______
New equity additions	______	______
Total cash available (A)	______	______
Cash Out		
Cash costs	______	______
Owners' salaries	______	______
Asset purchases	______	______
Principal payments	______	______
Owners' taxes and Social Security	______	______
Total cash spent (B)	______	______
(A) – (B) is closing cash balance	______	______

Figure 9.9. *A basic cash flow layout*

Item	July			January to July		
	Predict	Actual	Difference	Predict	Actual	Difference
Sales	40,000	0	(40,000)	300,000	240,000	8% down
Costs	30,000	32,000	2,000	200,000	205,000	3% up
Salary	3,000	3,000	0	21,000	24,000	14% up
Principal payment	5,000	0	(5,000)	30,000	25,000	17% down

Figure 9.10. *Example of the cash flow statement (in thousand $)*

normal business risks. The cash flow helps in thinking through this process. A good cash flow shows more than just predictions. It also shows the actuals, side by side with the predictions.

Figure 9.10 shows the next step. The first column lists the row names (items) as before. The second, third, and fourth columns list the predicted cash flow, the actual cash flow, and the difference between them for the current month (July). The final three columns list these same cash flow measures for the year to date. The idea behind these comparisons is not to overreact to temporary events when the firm is basically still on track. Thus decisions should be made from the last column (difference for the year to date) rather than the monthly difference column.

For example, there were no sales in July when the prediction was $40,000. This could be alarming, but the last set of columns show that the firm is only 8% down on the whole year so far, including this past month. So if the product was not quite ready for sale in July, then there is not much to worry about. These predictions are pretty good, but it would be another story if there were other reasons for no sales in July, such as poor quality or price falls. Costs are also well predicted. The reason for no principal payments is that there were no sales. The only problem with these numbers is that salary is higher than predicted, and this needs to be watched.

It is probably more useful to use percentages than numbers to express the differences between predicted and actuals. Percentages summarize the differences better. For example, a reduction in sales of $1 million looks startling, but if it is equivalent to a 3% drop, it does not seem so bad. The essential purpose of the cash flow is to make decisions when predicting it and when analyzing the differences between the predictions and the actuals.

Producing, reviewing, and using a cash flow are among the hardest tasks a manager does. But because cash is so vital today, these tasks also bring the highest reward. Budgeting right is managing right. No one in the firm can do the job right unless it is the right job for the firm. And the cash flow is at the culmination of the right job.

References

Chapter 3: Enhancing Greenhouse Profitability through Improved Personnel Management

Arkin, Joseph. 1995. "Counting the Hours." *American Nurseryman,* May 1, 1995.

Arkin, Joseph. 1990. "Keeping Your Crew." *American Nurseryman,* October 1, 1990.

Banchard, Dr. 1992. "Job Descriptions." *Nursery Retailer,* September/October, 1992.

Barton, S. S., J. J. Haydu, R. A. Hinson, R. E. McNiel, T. D. Phillips, R. D. Powell, and F. E. Stegelin. 1993. *Establishing and Operating a Garden Center: Requirements & Costs.* Washington, DC: Garden Centers of America.

Beytes, Chris and Joli A. Shaw. 1996. "How do your salaries compare?" *GrowerTalks,* October 1996.

Carpenter, Edwin D. 1991. "Finding and Keeping Employees." *Yankee Nursery Quarterly,* Spring 1991.

Cuculi, Karla Raye. 1995. "Labor Problems Force a Philosophy Change." *PRO,* January 1995.

Friedman, Harry. 1995. "Drive Your Rules Home." *Nursery Retailer,* November/December 1995.

Griggs, Judson. 1992. "Hiring Leadership." *American Nurseryman,* June 15, 1992.

Harlass, Sherry. 1994. "8 Ways to Recruit Good People to Work at Your Place of Business." *Nursery Manager,* January 1994.

Higginbotham, J. S. 1992. "Train for Success." *American Nurseryman,* August 1, 1992.

Lowndes, Leil. 1997. "Power to the People." *American Nurseryman,* May 1, 1997.

Manzel, K. E. 1996. "What Should I Pay? What Should I Earn?" *American Nurseryman,* October 15, 1996.

Marciel, R. 1994. "How to Hire Employees." *Nursery Manager,* January 1991.

Martinez, H. 1995. "Getting More for Less." *Nursery Management & Production,* February 1995.

Perry, P. M. 1997. "Confronting the No-Show." *American Nurseryman,* January 15, 1997.

Perry, P. M. 1994. "On Legal Grounds…When Hiring." *American Nurseryman,* May 1, 1994.

Perry, P. M. 1993. "Terminating Employees." *American Nurseryman,* January 15, 1993.

Powell, R. 1993. "How Much Do Your Employees Really Cost?" *Green Business Reporter,* Vol. 5, No. 6.

Powell, R. "Motivating Employees to Excel." *Penn State Cooperative Extension.*

Robinson, E. and A. Roberts. 1996. "Incentives Raise Skill and Morale." *Greenhouse Business,* October 1996.

Silber, K. 1992. "Perfecting Your Hiring Process." *American Nurseryman,* February 1, 1992.

Steele, J. 1992. "Reducing Turnover Through Effective Hiring." *The Landscape Contractor,* April 1992.

Steingold, Fred. 1997. "The How-to of Employee Handbooks." *American Nurseryman,* March 15, 1997.

Swartz, J. B. 1995. "Three Phases of the Employer-Employee Relationship." *The Public Garden,* October 1995.

Chapter 5: Enhancing Greenhouse Profitability through Improved Materials Handling and Distribution

Aylsworth, J. D. 1997. "Making It to Market." *Greenhouse Grower* 15(4):72,73,76,78.

Cuny, H. 1997. "Cooperative Shipping." *Nursery Management and Production* 13(12):20–23.

Davis, T. 1998a. "6 Ways to Improve Plant Keeping Ability." *Greenhouse Management and Production* 18(4): 31,32,34.

Davis, T. 1998b. "How to Streamline Shipping." *Greenhouse Management and Production* 18(4):20–25.

Hammer, P. A. 1998. "Cutting Labor in the Greenhouse." *GrowerTalks* 61(14):38–42.

Hopkins, M. 1998. "Loaded for Customer Service." *Greenhouse Grower* 16(1):134.

McLean, J. 1997. "Greenhouse Carts." *Greenhouse Management and Production* 17(4):40,42.

Ooykaas, D. E. 1998. "Weighing the Charges." *American Nurseryman* 187(6):44–45.

Socha, L. H. 1997. "Carts on a Roll." *Greenhouse Grower* 15(3):24–25.

Other Books from NRAES

The books below can be ordered from NRAES (Natural Resource, Agriculture, and Engineering Service). Complete book descriptions are posted on the NRAES Web site. The Web page address for each book is given below its description. Before ordering, contact NRAES for current prices and shipping and handling charges, or for a free catalog.

NRAES, Cooperative Extension
PO Box 4557
Ithaca, New York 14852-4557
Phone: (607) 255-7654
Fax: (607) 254-8770
E-mail: NRAES@CORNELL.EDU
Web site: WWW.NRAES.ORG

Features

- 53 illustrations
- 26 tables
- Sample calculations

ENERGY CONSERVATION FOR COMMERCIAL GREENHOUSES

Revision • NRAES–3 • 84 pages • 2001
ISBN 0-935817-74-3

Offers practical discussions of heat loss, site selection, construction materials, insulation, heating, ventilation, cooling, space utilization, trucking costs, and more. Also includes energy conservation checklist and useful conversion factors. Intended for greenhouse owners, designers, and educators.

WWW.NRAES.ORG/PUBLICATIONS/NRAES3.HTML

Features

- Capital budgets
- 15 tables
- Example businesses

ESTABLISHING AND OPERATING A GARDEN CENTER: Requirements and Costs

NRAES–161 • 66 pages • 2002
ISBN 0-935817-86-7

This revision discusses planning, capital investments, product mixes, labor, customers, layouts, pricing, advertising, and financial analysis. Analyzes example businesses with annual cash flows of $1,000,000 and $350,000. For potential and current garden center owners, their advisors, educators, and researchers.

WWW.NRAES.ORG/PUBLICATIONS/NRAES161.HTML

Features

- 105 illustrations
- 38 tables
- Sample calculations

GREENHOUSE ENGINEERING

NRAES–33 • 212 pages • 1994
ISBN 0-935817-57-3

Eight chapters and 13 appendixes include information needed to plan, construct, and manage a commercial greenhouse. Types of structures, materials handling equipment, environmental control, remodeling, and energy conservation are discussed. Intended for growers, designers, educators, and students.

WWW.NRAES.ORG/PUBLICATIONS/NRAES33.HTML

Features

- 150+ line drawings
- Sample calculations
- Greenhouse plans

GREENHOUSES FOR HOMEOWNERS AND GARDENERS

Revision • NRAES–137 • 200 pages • 2000
ISBN 0-935817-51-4

Eight chapters cover selecting a greenhouse plan or kit, construction planning, framing materials, glazing, layouts, equipment, environmental control, window greenhouses, growth chambers, and garden structures. Useful to gardeners, homeowners, educators, small farmers, retirement homes, schools, and other institutions.

WWW.NRAES.ORG/PUBLICATIONS/NRAES137.HTML

Features

- 37 illustrations
- 45 tables
- Glossary

HERBACEOUS PERENNIALS PRODUCTION: A Guide from Propagation to Marketing

NRAES–93 • 208 pages • 1998
ISBN 0-935817-29-8

Provides practical management information, including propagation methods for over 900 species, germination conditions for over 400 species, and common pest problems for over 400 species. Discusses several production systems and much more. Intended for growers, their advisors, and educators.

WWW.NRAES.ORG/PUBLICATIONS/NRAES93.HTML

Features

- 56 illustrations
- 32 tables
- 22,000+ sold

ON-FARM COMPOSTING HANDBOOK

NRAES–54 • 186 pages • 1992
ISBN 0-935817-19-0

Internationally recognized, practical book discusses large-scale composting, including raw materials, methods, equipment, management, marketing, and more. Includes worksheets, forms, and references. Intended for persons interested in large-scale composting, this book is also used as a college text.

WWW.NRAES.ORG/PUBLICATIONS/NRAES54.HTML

Features

- 100+ photos and illustrations
- 24 informative tables
- Equipment supplier lists

PRODUCTION OF VEGETABLES, STRAWBERRIES, AND CUT FLOWERS USING PLASTICULTURE

NRAES–133 • 156 pages • 2004
ISBN 0-935817-87-5

Covers plastic mulch, drip irrigation, fertigation, season extension, windbreaks, crop establishment, weed management, soil sanitation, and managing used plastics. Strawberry and cut flower production systems are described in depth. For new and experienced growers, educators, and serious gardeners.

WWW.NRAES.ORG/PUBLICATIONS/NRAES133.HTML

Backlist Titles

The Commercial Storage of Fruits, Vegetables, and Florist and Nursery Stocks

USDA–66 • 130 pages • 1986

WWW.NRAES.ORG/PUBLICATIONS/USDA66.HTML

Facilities for Roadside Markets

NRAES–52 • 32 pages • 1992

WWW.NRAES.ORG/PUBLICATIONS/NRAES52.HTML

Greenhouse Systems: Automation, Culture, and Environment

Conference Proceedings
NRAES–72 • 306 pages • 1994

WWW.NRAES.ORG/PUBLICATIONS/NRAES72.HTML

Proceedings of the XIIIth International Symposium on Horticultural Economics

Conference Proceedings
ACTA–429 • 600 pages • 1996

WWW.NRAES.ORG/PUBLICATIONS/ACTA429.HTML

Water and Nutrient Management for Greenhouses

NRAES–56 • 102 pages • 1996

WWW.NRAES.ORG/PUBLICATIONS/NRAES56.HTML

Workforce Management for Farms and Horticultural Businesses: Finding, Training, and Keeping Good Employees

Conference Proceedings
NRAES–117 • 140 pages • 1999
ISBN 0-935817-37-9

WWW.NRAES.ORG/PUBLICATIONS/NRAES117.HTML

Several NRAES books have won excellence awards from ASAE, the Society for Engineering in Agricultural, Food, and Biological Systems; ASHS, the American Society for Horticultural Science; or associations of cooperative extension educators. Books that have won one or more of these awards are designated by the blue ribbon symbol.

About NRAES

NRAES, the Natural Resource, Agriculture, and Engineering Service, is a not-for-profit program dedicated to assisting land grant university faculty and others in increasing the public availability of research- and experience-based knowledge. NRAES is sponsored by fourteen land grant universities in the eastern United States (see map below). We receive administrative support from Cornell University, the host university.

When you buy books from NRAES, you are helping to improve the accessibility of land grant university knowledge. While 15% of NRAES' annual income is provided by member universities, the funds to publish new books and coordinate new conferences come from our customers through book sales, conference registrations, and occasional project-specific grants.

NRAES publishes practical books of interest to fruit and vegetable growers, landscapers, dairy and livestock producers, natural resource managers, SWCD (soil and water conservation district) staff, consumers, landowners, and professionals interested in agricultural waste management and composting. NRAES books are used in cooperative extension programs, in college courses, as management guides, and for self-directed learning.

NRAES publishes two types of books: peer-reviewed books and conference proceedings. Our peer-reviewed books are evaluated prior to publication for technical accuracy and usefulness to the intended audience. The reviewers may include university faculty, extension educators, potential users, and interested persons from government and agribusiness. Conference proceedings are not peer-reviewed. However, the authors of papers presented at NRAES-sponsored conferences are chosen for their recognized expertise. NRAES also distributes some videos related to waste management and fruit and vegetable production.

NRAES was started in 1974 and was originally known as the Northeast Regional Agricultural Engineering Service. In 1987, with encouragement from member university extension directors, NRAES began offering its services to faculty from all disciplines at member universities. In 1998, Virginia Polytechnic Institute and State University joined the original thirteen member universities. Our name was changed in 1998 to reflect the expansion of NRAES beyond the Northeast and the broadening scope of our books and conferences.

Contact us for more information or a book catalog:

Natural Resource, Agriculture, and Engineering Service (NRAES)
Cooperative Extension
PO Box 4557
Ithaca, New York 14852-4557
Phone: (607) 255-7654
Fax: (607) 254-8770
E-mail: nraes@cornell.edu
Web site: www.nraes.org

Marty Sailus, NRAES Director
Jeffrey S. Popow, NRAES Managing Editor

NRAES Member Universities

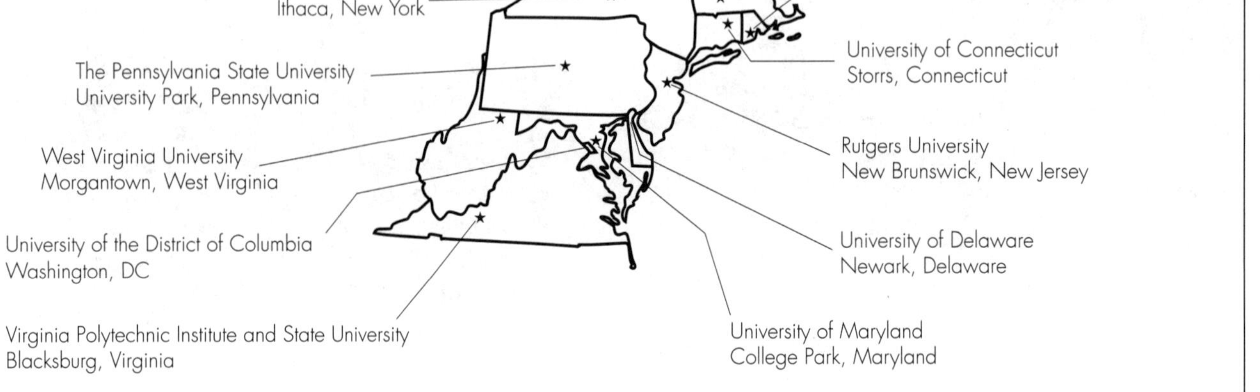